SURROUNDED BY
AWESOME WOMEN

SURROUNDED BY AWESOME WOMEN

UNLOCKING A NEW MODEL OF WOMEN'S SUCCESS
IN BUSINESS AND ENTREPRENEURSHIP
FOR THE NEXT DECADE

SHEILA LONG

NEW DEGREE PRESS

SURROUNDED BY AWESOME WOMEN

Unlocking a New Model of Women's Success in Business and Entrepreneurship for the Next Decade

ISBN   978-1-63676-819-9 *Paperback*
          978-1-63730-223-1 *Kindle Ebook*
          978-1-63730-263-7 *Ebook*

This book is dedicated to Thomas P. Leisle Jr., who devoted his life to helping others succeed in the hopes of building a stronger community. His individual efforts provided a collective benefit to the people around him, the community, and countless other individuals. Tom encouraged visionaries to persevere and connected them to key resources. In doing so, he ensured their ideas became reality, incredible partnerships formed, and authentic friendships blossomed. Tom was a selfless individual whose sole goal was to help others and for this I will be forever grateful.

We will see you again at the Meetup my friend.

Thomas P. Leisle, Jr.
February 8, 1953 – May 29, 2019

Contents

Introduction

HIP LADY AT THE END OF THE HALL

As I dropped off my two kindergartners in the school hallway, a woman stood at the end of the hall dressed impeccably in a tailored suit with fashionable heels. She was fellow parent Amanda Baltz, mother of four children, age six and under. She had performed a miracle in my eyes; her hair, nails, makeup, and jewelry were not only done, but looked impressive at 8 a.m. Amanda was going to be the school's Career Day presenter. She was going to teach the students how an incredible businesswoman operated, and I was thrilled.

Shortly afterward, Amanda and I became friends. From that day in 2012, I watched her grow a health care start-up into a cardiac diagnostic system partner for top health care systems. As she grew her business quietly, she practiced her faith and planned fun activities revolving around charity. Amanda did it in a balanced and healthy way while accepting that she cannot be everything to everyone.

What struck me about Amanda is that she was never competitive or territorial. On the contrary, she was always welcoming. While speaking at events, Amanda greeted friends, told the audience about her struggles with work-life balance and how she did not do it all at home and at school. Her realistic feedback left the audience spellbound, and through it all, Amanda remained herself. During the 2020 pandemic when her company's product was in dire need, she forged key health care and marketing partnerships, yet reached out when she heard I was writing a book to congratulate me.

Amanda and I not only were both parents with multiple children in the same school, but we both had a background on the business end of technology, and both became business owners. As I opened MalamaDoe: A Coworking Community for Women in 2017, I conducted two years of research as an avenue to connect women.[1] Over time, I met many women unfamiliar with how to operate a business and documented the common roadblocks they had, including facing fears, accepting realities, building brands, and scaling businesses into an incubator model. I noticed how women's sensitive emotional states, feelings about financing, and progress with personal branding differed. I then developed a roadmap for women business owners and created an incubator called the Awesome Women Incubator Model, which I detail in this book. Here is the story of how it came to be.

---

1   "Our Story," MalamaDoe, accessed March 29, 2021.

MY STORY

I had a successful career in technology in the 1990s and early 2000s, where I worked in a heavily male-dominated industry of telecommunications. My company had been a leader in assisting women professionally and I had grown my career steadily over a decade there. I held varying levels of responsibility and thrived professionally. Unfortunately, although I had a bright future, it was stalled when I became ill with a debilitating health condition. I was advised that if I wanted to successfully bear multiple children, I needed to leave the workforce for the time being. I became a stay-at-home mother after the birth of my first child. I tell this story more in depth in **Chapter One**.

To prepare for this lifestyle change, I returned to my home state in a new city within a smaller market. I moved closer to my family as a transplant, knowing I would have to eventually start over professionally. In this new location, no one knew me as a career woman and the scarce flexible work options and part-time positions available demonstrated the proliferation of institutional sexism, especially to newcomers considered overqualified. Years later, when I was done with childbearing and ready to return to the workforce, I reached out to my network of mothers for professional connections to no avail. Sadly, women felt powerless and had muffled stories of how basic career needs could not be met as a result of institutional betrayal, discussed more in **Chapter Five,** that permeated the workplace. I realized all the years of experience in my field, rank in the company and industry, and a network of mothers in my neighborhood would provide no benefit to me and I would have to own my path as a business owner.

Thankfully, I had attended and graduated from an MBA program in Chicago and returned there for a few days to meet with some key personnel. I met with Kelly O'Brien in their Career Services Department and told her I hadn't worked in many years and needed a safe, balanced workplace environment. I acknowledged I had an unstable marriage and lived in a neighborhood where I was surrounded by awesome women who were also disconnected professionally and needed personal balance.

Kelly told me I was not alone in feeling isolated, incomplete, and inadequate because I was lacking professional resources and support, afraid I would not reach my full potential. She challenged me to return home and help women in my neighborhood. By following my drive to start a business, she advised me to give these women the needed access to autonomous convenient tools and professional networks.

I did just as she recommended. Over the past six years, I have met hundreds of women worldwide seeking professional connections looking to stop history in its tracks and listened as they refused to allow a dismal future for the next generation of women to continue. As they struggled with having a diminishing personal and professional brand, I heard their stories of being blindsided by microaggressions stemming from a lack of executive presence and cultural and network power, alongside demeaning and demanding stereotypes related to their femininity. It was clear women, because of the gender imbalance, were surrounded by institutional sexism and betrayal. They must own their own path as business owners. I delve into these concerns in:

- **Chapter Seven** on sexism
- **Chapter Eight** on the macro effects of microaggressions due to the gender imbalance
- **Chapter Nine** on culture, power, and femininity stereotypes
- **Chapter Ten** on executive presence and confidence

I listened to these stories within the safe community which I founded, MalamaDoe: A Coworking Community for Women. Here I created a haven filled with empathetic, caring, and courageous individuals where they know they will belong and thrive.

SMALL BUSINESS FACTS

Woman who are shunned professionally must feel and accept uncomfortable emotions, such as shame. When facing and owning those emotions, a woman comes out on the other side thriving as an empowered business owner and owns her path forward. As women build businesses, we forge a new path where sound decision-making, empathy, and compassion are appreciated. We evaluate what truly works for us and recreate ourselves professionally as we face fears, accept our realities, build our brands, and scale our businesses.

Small business ownership is on the rise in the United States, with the US Small Business Administration Office of Advocacy Small Business Profile reporting a 9.1 percent increase in growth from 28.8 million in 2013 to 31.7 million in 2019.[2]

---

2 U.S. Small Business Administration Office of Advocacy, "United States Small Business Report, 2019" (Washington DC: Small Business Administration, 2019).

Yet, the noteworthy fact is that women-owned businesses are rising even faster than their male counterparts.

Small businesses are the engine of the world's economy. Studies by The Kauffman Index, which since 1996 "was among the most requested and far-reaching entrepreneurship research in the United States, and, arguably, the world" validate how women have opened, and continue to open, small businesses at a rate much faster than men.[3] Another key resource is the Annual State of Women-Owned Businesses Report, commissioned by American Express, which found that women do not grow their skills as rapidly as men if a more inclusive type of support is not provided.[4]

BUSINESS OWNERSHIP HELPS WOMEN HEAL, THRIVE, & CELEBRATE OUR STRENGTHS

By creating the supportive community within my business, MalamaDoe, society and women can flourish while attaining personal balance and safety. In doing so, women feel fulfilled and receive energetic encouragement and support to build businesses while reaching objectives. Women thrive as society witnesses their transformation into a place of peace, stability, and self-acceptance. As we elevate our businesses, we create structural change in areas that traditionally hamper women's professional growth, including microaggressions inherent in institutional sexism and betrayal.

---

3   Ewing Marion Kauffman Foundation, "Historical Kauffman Index," accessed January 15, 2021.

4   American Express, *The 2019 State of Women-Owned Business Report* (New York: American Express, 2019), 3-10.

Women's business ownership became notable in the US Census Bureau in 1972, making it "the year related to female entrepreneurship."[5] Since this year, women worldwide have grown their ownership of business from 4.6 percent to 36 percent. Since 1997 to 2017, women-owned businesses were opened 2.5 percent higher than the "national average when male-owned business is taken into account" with a 467 percent growth rate in the quantity of firms opened.[6]

As our population ages and women outlive men, new sponsors will provide funding and training that truly supports women entrepreneurs.[7] As women and sponsors collaborate, female mentorship will blossom because women will define new definitions of success.[8] Women's lives are full of many moving pieces, and they must gingerly navigate them to ensure a successful outcome. Often, they travel down a zigzagged path while working toward personal and professional goals. Instead of winning and competing, women take courageous steps forward that focus on continual improvement.[9] In doing so, they become an inspiration, forging collaborative partnerships with women-led groups worldwide.

5   Branka Vuleta, "22 Mind-Blowing Women Entrepreneurs Statistics," *What To Become* (blog), August, 11, 2020.

6   Andrea Stonjanovic, "Ladies Who Lead - 35+ Amazing Women in Business Statistics," *Small Biz Genius* (blog), updated December 2, 2020, accessed March 27, 2021.

7   Esteban Ortiz-Ospina and Diana Beltekian, "Why Do Women Live Longer than Men?," *Our World in Data* (blog), August 14, 2018, accessed March 27, 2021.

8   Geri Stengel, "How Women Entrepreneurs Are Redefining Wealth Management," *Forbes*, March 27, 2019.

9   Rieva Kesonsky, "The State of Women Entrepreneurs," *Score* (blog), March 24, 2020, accessed March 27, 2021.

That day in the hall when I saw Amanda, I wondered if she was unique, or part of a world I didn't know. She was a piece of how this book came to be. As I witnessed Amanda's business grow, I forged friendships with other women, some running businesses and some former business owners. I also met with women who were contemplating starting a business, had grown an idea into a viable business, or had achieved incredible success. Over time, I built a community of women business owners, and we became colleagues.

With each new colleague, I noticed some common trends for how women incubate businesses. In six years' time, I transformed this information into the Awesome Women Incubator Model. I wrote this book to distribute my findings and create a path for women to recreate themselves professionally by launching, growing, and running businesses with a tool that gives them what they are missing and saves them time. With this model, women can put their professional career back on track by courageously forging a path forward and reaching their full potential while creating a better future for the next generation of women.

HELPING WOMEN GROW WITH THE INCUBATOR MODEL

In a community setting, women assess and reassess what works for them, finding a personal and professional fit that enables them to grow. Women celebrate working together alongside colleagues while using their strengths to the fullest.

In areas where collaboration is not a core value, a woman's efforts to work collectively while setting personal boundaries may not be appreciated. If a competitive leadership structure results in long hours, she may face insurmountable ceilings and institutional betrayal. She may feel she does not belong and experience territorialism, which is delved into more in **Chapter Six**. Alongside this new reality, she leaves to champion a better future.

Running MalamaDoe and working with female business owners, I have witnessed women's business growth while they celebrate their awesome strengths. Today we see this happen, both virtually and in person, with mom's groups, school and equity organizations, and in women-only coworking spaces across the world.

We know celebrating other women is nothing new. It has happened for centuries. Women need other women to keep moving forward so that we can all thrive. On that note, I share with you my findings for what I have formulated in the Awesome Women Incubator Model from my interviews initially with forty-one female business owners in **Chapter Two**. As I created the model, I documented similar milestones women met as they launched and grew businesses. I placed them into categories and applied them to the different tiers of where they fit in the business in terms of growth. Over the next few years, I tested out the findings with women who attended speaking events and toured my business, realizing the results were quite accurate.

As women launch and grow businesses, they must understand the role of their emotional state and feelings about finances. The Awesome Women model understands these feelings are normal for women as they run businesses and sets expectations for the present and future.

My model is easily relatable. For example, in the first two tiers, **Discovery** and **Canvasser,** a woman lays the groundwork for her company and I delve into how people in:

- **Chapter One,** leave situations where they lack financial fulfillment or support
- **Chapter Three,** seek a supportive work culture as a Flexibility, Necessity, or Opportunity Entrepreneur, or Sideprenuer
- **Chapter Four,** proactively work toward work-life balance with a tool such as the Wheel of Life
- **Chapter Five,** recognize the repercussions of unsettling betrayal and territorialism
- **Chapter Six,** fill out the Business Model Canvas

As a woman builds her business, she heals, thrives, and celebrates her strengths as she evolves into the tiers of **Growth, Prosperer, Fulfillment,** and **Expansion.** Here, while entrenched in running the daily operations of a business, she celebrates similar and different milestones when selling, networking, and funding businesses. Because of these similarities in each tier and her own unique differences, women business owners carve their own path toward success in business and entrepreneurship.

There are trends that create empowered women. Women have mastered the side hustle—working multiple jobs at one time—and now have multiple streams of income. Women have dominated the service industry and have the potential to drastically change the landscape in the emerging social impact space. I am reminded of a quote from Malala Yousafzai.

"I raise up my voice—not so that I can shout, but so that those without a voice can be heard. We cannot all succeed when half of us are held back."[10]

Women need to find work they enjoy and walk down a path that helps them flourish. They are in a part of history where businesswomen lift up fellow women, where business owners support colleagues who are black, Indigenous and people of color, or BIPOC, by putting racial equity frameworks in place at their businesses and actively act to improve upon them.

I wrote this book to unlock the potential of entrepreneurial women, understanding that everyone plays a part in their success. By reading this book, you can do your part in creating a better future for women. This book is for:

- Young women and seasoned professionals alike, both who are healing from broken personal and professional dreams. As they seek motivation to move forward with their careers, they will find the needed encouragement to follow a path less traveled and take charge of their own destiny.
- Caretakers for youth, elderly, sick, and special people.

---

10   Harpers Bazaar Staff, "60 Empowering Feminist Quotes from Inspiring Women," *Harper Bazaar*, February 28, 2020.

- Career changers looking for a clear path and business owners seeking camaraderie. In it, they will find a roadmap they can follow to grow their businesses complete with key milestones. They will gain an understanding of the typical emotions faced at each step of business ownership.
- Family members and women's allies seeking to better understand the impact of gender inequality on the women in their lives.

By reading and empathizing with women's perspectives, this book will give supporters a toolkit to actively support women personally and professionally.

HOW THIS BOOK WILL HELP YOU

This book is written out of deference and respect to women trailblazers and those impacted and inspired by their leadership. By reading this book, women and their allies will better understand how to create empowering workspaces. You will hear stories of over forty female entrepreneurs and understand the actual terms that define each entrepreneurial type and why a woman falls into each category.

You will gather insights from women who

- faced unwelcome workplaces where they were not professionally connected
- passed through turning points in their life without resources or support
- experienced microaggressions alongside demanding femininity stereotypes

When women's basic needs are not being met because of the gender imbalance and the inappropriate behavior that results in institutional sexism and betrayal, they must own their own path as a business owner. As professional business growth is stifled because they do not have autonomous access to flexible and convenient tools and professional networks, they feel isolated, incomplete, and inadequate. As women lack resources to get back on track, they fear they may never reach their full potential and thus reside in an anxious space. Yet, women courageously forge a path forward and each has a story to tell. This book celebrates awesome women in our midst, while giving a clear understanding of why they are starting businesses at historic rates, how their definition of success changes based on where they fall in the Awesome Woman Incubator Model, and what is normal for women at each tier of running a business, from Discovery to Expansion.

PART ONE

BREAKING THROUGH

CHAPTER ONE

Brusque Endings Create New Professional Realities

ONE FATEFUL DAY

"Oh! My fingers hurt!" I set down the phone into its cradle and gently soothed my swollen knuckles. I had picked it up ready to dial a friend to share my elation of a major professional win, but my fingers hurt too much to dial the phone number. Instead, I stared at my desk where I was a manager in a Fortune 100 communication company and contemplated the situation. I guessed I could've dialed with the tip of a pen, but was it worth it? My fingers were pretty important and needed some attention.

I noticed my fingers had been hard to move lately, and, while focusing on doing my job, I had been ignoring them as I didn't want my health to deter me. Also, my ankles had been swollen for a while. Every day I noticed it was worse. That day I could not wear shoes and resorted to boots because of the excessive swelling.

How had this uncontrollable situation happened? I was challenged at work, moving up in the company, had a fun social life, and was engaged to be married. Under pressure as each required balance, I realized support was lacking. Notably, my work environment was fraught with incredible uncertainty with constant layoffs. Also, the department I managed delivered a high-stress, demanding service. When I became their leader, I noticed my staff had poor boundaries related to work-life balance and definitely lacked support and fulfillment. I witnessed how those working in the department were experiencing what researchers Fernando Bartolomé and Paul A. Lee Evans, who investigated and interviewed more than two thousand managers and their wives, coined as negative emotional spillover. In a nutshell, it is when someone brings the negativity from the office home with them and it impacts not only their personal life, but those near and dear to them.[11]

Because of the anxiety and uncertainty going on at the company, I did what I believe every manager should in times of crisis and massive layoffs; I took over and shielded my staff from whatever company politics I could.[12] Simultaneously, I implemented process changes that transformed the delivery of our service from a high to a low-stress environment.

WOMEN'S FIGHT FOR EQUALITY

Looking at my situation, even though it lacked balance and support, I realized how far women have come over the past five decades. Growing up in the 1970s, women transformed

---

11 Fernando Bartolomé and Paul A. Lee Evans, "Why Must Success Cost So Much?" *Harvard Business Review*, March 1980.
12 Ibid.

the world for me. They stood up for their rights, demanded change, withstood unfair treatment, and became tough fighters for the next generation of women. They made inroads garnering more respect professionally as the rules were modified at small and large companies. These women were, are, and will continue to be my heroes.[13]

When women entered businesses, big and small, in the 1970s and 1980s, companies needed to adapt to meet their needs. Now, a half a century later, some still have not adapted. Nowhere is this clearer than with the pay gap. The pay gap showcases the inequities in pay as women earn far less than their male counterparts, at eight-two cents to a man's dollar in earnings.[14] Some noteworthy fields where the pay gap is glaringly evident are those of female personal financial advisors, where women earn 59 percent less than men, female administrative service managers, where women earn 62 percent less than men, female emergency medical technicians and paramedics, where women earn 66 percent less than men, and sales, where women earn 67 percent less than men.[15] Employees impacted by the pay gap in firms and industries that do not address it suffer.[16] Because of compensation discrimination, outdated companies operate in a world where only certain workers flourish professionally, emotionally, and financially.

---

13   Ryan Bergeron, "'The Seventies': Feminism Makes Waves," *CNN*, August 17, 2015.

14   Amanda Fins, *Women and the Lifetime Wage Gap: How Many Woman Years Does It Take to Equal 40 Man Years?* (Washington, DC: National Women's Law Center, 2020), 1-2.

15   Samuel Stebbins and Thomas C. Frohlich, "20 Jobs with the Largest Gender Pay Gap for Women," *USA Today*, December 8, 2018.

16   Cory Stieg, "How the Gender Pay Gap Affects Women's Mental Health," *CNBC*, March 31, 2020.

THE DOCTOR WEIGHS IN

The stress had caught up with me, and as I attempted to make this phone call, I realized my health was now suffering. I gently picked up the phone and dialed my doctor, who told me a visit to a rheumatologist was in order. I set up an appointment for the next day with a doctor who had an opening. The next morning, my newfound doctor took two minutes to examine me.

"Hi. My name is Dr. Lert. Do not try to pronounce my full name. Just call me Dr. Lert. Show me your hands. Now your feet. Look at your ankles! Try and move them. Now the shoulders. Lift your arms. Oh, you cannot lift them more? Okay. Try harder. Wow, you really cannot bend your elbow. Why you wait so long to come see me?"

I dreaded his reply. "Can you fix this? I was hoping it would go away."

"Maybe, I can fix this. You are now one of my patients." He informed me I had rheumatoid arthritis and that he knew a lot about that. "You are lucky you know me. I think I can fix this. We have to wait and see. You just need to take this medication. Now, very important to go get it now. Then, you come back in one week, then in three weeks, then in five weeks and you should be back to normal. We hope. We wait and we see."

I was beside myself with relief as the medication would miraculously reverse the signs of arthritis that had formed. If all went well, my joint movement would return. I listened as he added, "Now just one thing. No babies. That would be very bad. So, no babies."

Shocked by what I was hearing, I stopped dead in my tracks. I wondered to myself, how could this be happening? I was thirty years old and knew the clock was ticking. With every year passing and a child not being conceived, the risks of having a healthy baby with birth defects increased. I asked him to repeat himself, hoping it was a language barrier. "Excuse me?"

Dr. Lert repeated, "Babies are very bad. You need to fix your joints now. No babies. We wait and we see."

As I heard this diagnosis and the subsequent restriction, my mind was reeling with the injustice of it all. Because I constantly sought equilibrium of calm amidst the chaos at work, I had become physically ill with a disease that would always be with me and now I had been told may not be able to bear children.

"When will this go away? I cannot have a baby? Ever?"

Shaking his head, Dr. Lert repeated, "You come in one week, then in three weeks, then in five weeks. You are very lucky you know me. We wait and we see."

I reflected on how this diagnosis would not impact the career of a man: he would be able to take medication and continue working while moving up the career ladder, making more of an impact professionally all while increasing his pay. He would not need to choose between taking care of his body to bear children or to continue in his field. Yet, because of my gender, my world would be impacted. It was so unjust.

SURVIVING IN STEM

At work, my career was skyrocketing; after years of climbing the corporate ladder, I was forging relationships by elevating my staff. I had persevered. Just as what the book *Brotopia: Breaking Up the Boys' Club of Silicon Valley* said, I had "moved into a position of real influence" yet was still viewed as close enough in age to my coworkers in their twenties to get real work done.[17]

I happily worked alongside my female colleagues who achieved balance and harmony in their lives. Yet, I realized they made choices to be there such as not being the caretaker even after the workday was over, having fewer children, which was more manageable, and having a support system to help them with the day-to-day operations of their lives. I knew they had figured out how to balance it all and I aspired to be like them.

I worked in a company surrounded by women in science, technology, engineering, and mathematics, or STEM. They, according to *Brotopia*, "were 807% more likely to leave their jobs than their peers in other fields," yet 32 percent of women didn't think they would last more than a year. Research shows that when women hit thirty and became mothers, they had to choose between maintaining a healthy marriage with "family demands" and work-life balance or working in STEM.[18]

I realized my coworkers' lack of long-term career longevity was because of prioritizing their families, a constant threat

17   Emily Chang, *Brotopia: Breaking Up the Boys' Club of Silicon Valley* (New York: Penguin Audio, 2018), Audible audio ed., 6 hr., 53 min.
18   Ibid.

of layoffs, and a resulting feeling of loneliness in Brotopia. Sadly, research confirms most women who exit STEM do not return. According to *Brotopia*, "after twelve years, 50 percent of women left jobs in STEM to work in other fields," in contrast to the 80 percent retention rate in other fields.[19]

I talked to my business coach, Elene Cafasso with Enerpace, Inc., about why women left and why I stayed.[20] I analyzed how the industry operated. It was dominated by technology projects, which must run according to the core principles of the project management triple constraint of running on time, within budget, and according to specifications. These requirements are always a challenge to meet. Yet, in areas where collaboration may not be the core value because of a competitive leadership structure, it can lead to long hours and institutional betrayal as the worker's collaborative nature and personal boundaries may not be valued by management because of insurmountable ceilings in place.

My coach Elene brought out her coaching tool, the Wheel of Life, which we used to measure life success and which we will look at more in **Chapter Four**. Unfortunately, the key areas measured on the Wheel of Life did not fare well for a woman in technology, or for any field where long hours in a male-dominated environment were required.

- When a woman is the primary breadwinner, she may not be a caretaker and be forced to work long hours and endure high stress to get ahead. Her life partner, if she

---

19   Ibid.
20   "Meet Our Team," Enerpace, accessed March 27, 2021.

has one, is then forced to take a back seat emotionally and professionally. She also has little time for fun, recreation, personal growth, romance, or friends and family, all of which impacts her health.

- At work, the employee faces institutional betrayal, discussed further in **Chapter Five**, and the reasoning behind the bias they feel as a misfit, which we look at more in **Chapter Six,** which stands in the way of their career mobility. Also, the women know the repercussions of the pay gap, where women do not get paid as much as men. Women see few examples of success stories in their future and have little balance, support, or fulfillment professionally.

Yet, in my case, I had stayed working in STEM. I had the drive to continue with the end goal of moving up in the company, and I had succeeded. For ten years, while working late hours, weekends, and going to after-work parties, I had met colleagues for drinks, participated in the social activities, and steered clear of department politics. I had volunteered to work on extra assignments and helped the company maintain its integrity and played my cards right. Now, finally, I was being rewarded.

On the personal side, I was engaged to be married. Things were all heading in the right direction where I could be the working mother who would break the glass ceiling in Corporate America. My husband and future kids would have a wife and mother they would be proud of, as I had defied the traditional mold of women. I thought I had the balance, support, and fulfillment needed, but my body disagreed.

I couldn't move my fingers or my feet, and apparently my elbows and shoulders were next. I had to make a tough choice, exit the corporate career ladder I had so diligently worked for, and repair my body and possibly become a biological mother or continue on my quest to shatter the glass ceiling for women in technology.

At that moment, sitting in front of the doctor, I looked into my heart and knew I wanted a better life. It was at this moment that I knew I was done. Done with corporate. Done with Women in Technology. Done with shattering a glass ceiling that we all knew would never be broken because of the inevitable repercussions of gender inequality. I decided I was going to focus on me. It was all about hope now, hope the raging swelling in my body would get under control, and hope for a different life.

Here is a story of another woman who was also at a crossroads in her career. She reached a different trajectory but had to make a tough choice as well.

LUCY'S DIRECT STYLE

Lucy was another top performer helping senior leadership merge two organizations. In her work, she partnered closely with human resource leaders. Lucy's outgoing manner and suggestions were very thought provoking and appreciated by her manager, the vice president of organizational development, yet they were not well received by the vice president of human resources. He did not like Lucy's direct style.

She would offer her ideas with trust and transparency, thinking her human resource colleagues would appreciate her collaboration, but the more she contributed, the more threatened her colleagues felt. At one point Lucy's manager asked her colleague, "If Lucy was a man would you be feeling this same way?" Lucy finally left the organization when her manager could not protect her any longer.

Her leader hated to see her go but was able to support her with a severance because of the conflict with the vice president of human resources. Despite her successes in this role and no performance issues, Lucy lost a lot of confidence working in this environment. She was recruited into a similar role for a competitor and thrived in a culture of high performance.

Yet, it took Lucy many years to recover her full confidence from this experience. She now runs her own business. She only works with people where there is mutual love and respect.

HELPING WOMEN THRIVE

Not advancing women professionally is a key driver of territorialism. Territorialism holds women back by letting our own personal concerns overshadow the need for women to progress professionally. It starts with making us question our choices, to falter in our "confidence" because we know the repercussions of our progress are too great and too much to bear personally. For this unfortunate cycle of societal and cultural expectations to break, we need for women, and their male counterparts, to stop this behavior in its tracks.

When we see a woman who has done everything right, or the majority right with a few missteps, we need to celebrate these awesome women. We need to welcome them to the arena where they may be the only woman there. We need to understand their differences from the mainstream and appreciate them, while wishing them well as they venture into uncharted territory.

Women entered businesses, big and small, in the 1970s and 1980s. Yet, these women tasked with doing it all could not deliver. Shopping, cooking, cleaning, caretaking, socializing, and entertaining took a toll on us all. The divorce rate skyrocketed, increasing from 20 percent in the 1950s to 50 percent in the 1970s.[21]

Yet, as the decades passed, women continued to fight for equality. The 2010s had been an epiphany of new insights into today's world for women. From the unearthing of information with the #MeToo and #TimesUp movement, clearly, there is a need to celebrate women. The dissatisfaction with how things were in the 1970s and 1980s is evident, yet many areas of concern continue to be unresolved. Here is the story of one such woman who devotes her life to justice. She is the least territorial person I know. She always champions women and elevates their voices.

JACKIE BECOMES A LAWYER

In 1981, Jackie Boynton was working in the child welfare area when the unfortunate ending of a man's life changed the course of hers. When Earnest Lacy died at the hands of the Milwaukee police, Jackie was asked to assist in his investigation. Although

---

21   W. Bradford Wilcox, "The Evolution of Divorce," *National Affairs*, Fall 2009, accessed March 31, 2021.

she did not work directly with the district attorney, the effort to ensure the response to police brutality was thorough and independent. It inspired her to apply to law school. Jackie had considered applying ten years prior but had not. She did so then and was accepted. At age thirty-five, Jackie returned to college to attend law school. She found she was a much older student than her classmates. Yet, Jackie persevered, graduated, and has had a varied thirty-five-year legal career. Jackie's business is in the Awesome Women's Tier of Fulfillment.

Jackie primarily has focused her time as a lawyer working in civil rights and employee law representing the plaintiff, and employee and labor law representing unions. She has served on many boards of directors in the Milwaukee area and also teaches nonprofit law at two local universities.

Jackie is a firm supporter of pro-choice women candidates running for office. Whether it be through Emily's List or Women Lead Wisconsin, she is a huge advocate of voting rights and celebrates initiatives which give women a stronger voice.[22] [23] Whatever is going on with the Democratic Party in town, Jackie normally has been consulted or invited. She is an inspiration to many.

RETURNING HOME AND BECOMING A STAY-AT-HOME MOM

After receiving my arthritis diagnosis, I made some changes to my role at work and moved back to my home state of

---

22 "Home," Emily's List, accessed February 6, 2021.
23 "Home," Women Lead Wisconsin, accessed February 6, 2021.

Wisconsin. This move increased my work commute from two to four hours daily. Eventually, I became pregnant and gave birth to a wonderful healthy baby girl. Upon returning home from the hospital, I opened my mail to discover I had been laid off, and, after my maternity leave, my first day back would be my last.

As a mother of a newborn, my main concern after caring for my family was to keep my arthritis at bay so I could stay off medication and conceive another child prior to the onset of the arthritis again, which had gone away during pregnancy. After discussing my situation with my doctors, it was apparent the best option was to become a stay-at-home mom until I was done with childbearing. So, out of the blue with no planning, I became a stay-at-home mom.

I was definitely a fish out of water in a home in the suburbs with a baby. I had worked for over a decade at the same company and lived in a large city, both of which were a big part of my identity. In my new location, I had my extended family who lived nearby and neighbors on my block as friends. Other than that, I had my husband and baby and knew no one else.

I went from a day-to-day reality of making process decisions that would impact two hundred plus people every few hours, to deciding about where to best locate the supplies near the changing table to avoid a mess or dangerous situation with a newborn. I went from choosing who to sit with at lunch in our seven hundred plus corporate cafeteria and which Indian, Mexican, or American entrees to eat, to enjoying leftovers sitting next to a sleeping baby while folding the laundry, making a grocery list, and planning our next outing so I could have a conversation with another adult that day. It was quite an adjustment.

Yet, the biggest adjustment was the role reversal in the home. With the long commute and additional responsibilities gone, I was actually in our house all the time and I was thrilled to be in charge. I greeted visitors to our home, hosted dinner parties and potlucks, and became the general contractor as we renovated our kitchen. I made our house a home.

Over the next four years, I bore two more children and witnessed playdates, children's milestones and cared for sick children. I did my best to keep my children safe while dressing them in well-fitting, gender-appropriate clothing. While focusing on keeping a calm demeanor, I did what I could to maintain happiness between three small children. I encouraged my husband to work long hours and to travel when asked. When he was gone for long periods, I hired a babysitter for nights out or swapped care with a friend. Otherwise, I resorted to having little help in the home to save money and preserve our privacy. I worked pro-bono as a consultant to stay active professionally while balancing life and home accordingly.

Over time, I made friends at local moms' groups and was relieved to talk over concerns about my children developmentally. Soon afterwards, I was invited to book clubs and family-friendly parties where I met more acquaintances and served on local boards. In these newfound friendships, I relished having people to lean on in times of need, and these friendships were, and still are, a huge part of my life. I realized my friends and I rarely had the same professional background and very few women I met were in business. Here is the story of one such friend who I did meet who worked in business.

NIKI THE TRAVEL ADVISOR

As a stay-at-home mom, thankfully I met a great friend in Niki Kremer. She worked in corporate travel as a travel agent for over two decades. Our kids were close in age and I was thrilled to meet a successful and happy working woman. Niki had contemplated opening her own travel agency over the years and she eventually moved forward with her plans, opening Via Travel Service.[24] Her news was well received by her family and Niki took baby steps to get her business moving as she entered the Awesome Woman Tier of Canvasser. Over time, Niki grew her business enough to have earned the money to open up an office to meet clients. She established her business's brand and became a bit of a celebrity, working primarily off of referrals. I currently place Niki in the Awesome Woman Tier of Prospering.

TOM LEISLE: TEAMWORK AND COLLABORATION

After the birth of my first child, I began working pro-bono for a local group as a consultant to businesses in Milwaukee. After working with them for over five years, I was ready for a new adventure. So, one morning after a final in-person meeting, I parted ways with them. As I got in my car after that meeting, I was a bit down. I had had made many connections

---

24 "About," Via Travel Service, accessed March 31, 2021.

with them, yet now I would have to start over again. I started my car and drove to a different meeting, which I had decided, at the onset of the day, to miss. But fate brought me there that day.

This second meeting was one that I had been periodically attending with a local entrepreneurial group with my sole goal being to network and begin consulting while developing an idea I had for a business. Unfortunately, as I drove there, I found myself stopped behind a train a few blocks from the meeting. With literally nowhere to go, I let myself feel the despair. I sat in my car seething that, once again, I would have to walk down a new path. I would walk into this meeting late and miss the only thing I needed, the networking session beforehand.

Yet, when I arrived, I realized I had been granted a gift. Today, the normal meeting format had changed and there was no speaker. Overjoyed, I realized I could network. Two of the organizers at the front of the room were expressing their disappointment about the low attendance for these meetings overall. They were asking for advice on what to do.

I spoke up. I recommended we introduce ourselves, state what we were looking to do, and ask for assistance. They agreed this would help and asked me to start. I began,

"My name is Sheila Long. I live in Shorewood, and I am sur-rounded by awesome, talented women in my neighborhood. I know their stories and how they have left the workplace to move to this city, Milwaukee. Now, they are unable to work because of the lack of part-time, flexible positions offered. I

want to create a group where these women can network in my village and build businesses."

The listeners in the room murmured a bit, and I was thrilled I stated my story and found the courage to actually say it out loud. Then, one by one, the meeting continued, and the group introduced themselves. We became more than connected; we became friends.

After the meeting, a very tall gentleman, about twenty years older than me, rushed over to me with an outstretched hand.

"Hi, Thomas P. Leisle, Jr." He pulled out his phone. "You want to help women. I want to help women. What's the city you want to open the business in? Shorewood?"

I answered, shocked I would actually get somewhere with my idea, "Yes, Shorewood."

"Give me a second. You want to rent it, right, not buy it?" We had met before, Tom and me. He was one of the speakers and knew everyone in the room. He explained, "I am a commercial realtor. I have a building for you. This is the best price you are going to find. Write down the address and give me an update next week."

The onlookers smiled, and no one was amazed. They just told me Tom would help me. That is definitely what Tom did, and those twenty seconds were just the beginning. He found me the location for my future business, and he followed up week after week on my progress.

What Tom had successfully done for me was to pull me out of the tier in my model, which I call Discovery, which is one where someone would like to start a business but doesn't move toward this goal. This tier is the most challenging to exit, and most never leave it. This tier takes an emotional toll.

Networking with the group that day made me accountable to moving ahead with my dream of uplifting my village, my city, and my home state by improving how women were treated professionally. I could now help females who needed professional resources and support.

ROLLING OUT MALAMADOE

I took my experience facilitating local panels and sitting on boards, my project management and Six Sigma training, and my background working for over eleven years at a Fortune 100 communications company in high-tech sales, quality, and service management to organize my business. I also returned to my roots at the newly founded Polsky Center at my alma mater, the University of Chicago Booth School of Business, for some great support on how to open a coworking space.[25] [26] The Polsky Center provided me with the training to better understand social innovation, and I used my learnings from my MBA in strategy and finance to define the strategy and fine-tune my projections.

---

25 "Home," Polsky Center for Entrepreneurship & Innovation, The University of Chicago, accessed February 6, 2021.

26 "Home," The University of Chicago Booth School of Business, accessed February 6, 2021.

I entered the Awesome Woman Tier of Canvasser as a Flexibility Entrepreneur.

I formally rolled out MalamaDoe: A Coworking Community for Women in May 2017, after planning for two years and when my children were old enough to enter full-day school. The name comes from a Hawaiian term, Malama, which means to care or to protect through stewardship in business. Since my goal was to create powerful women leaders in business who are community focused, it all came together in that name. The Doe came into play because of the hometown basketball team the Milwaukee Bucks.

Over the next seven months, I created an advisory council of which Tom and my brother Kevin were the most active members; they escorted me by the hand and helped me win without judgement or hatred. They were incredible mentors during an emotional time who stood by me while taking me out of my comfort zone.

MalamaDoe is a place that values flexibility and supports self-aware, compassionate, community-focused women. By creating this collaborative setting, which opened doors and leveled the playing field for women, I created an equalizer for females that was made to be intentionally engaging. My business made an impact, and I created it because I had people who walked the path with me while simultaneously going through the tiers of opening a business. From Niki Kremer, the corporate travel agent who had recently started her own business called Via Travel, to Jamie Lynn Tatera, an elementary school teacher launching a resilience and self-compassion business called Wholly Mindful, to Julia

Knox and Carey Vollmers, two women in the throes of a career change, we, and many others, all came together to build the futures of women in business.[27] [28]

Regardless of how our new professional reality came about, we took the reins of the opportunity at hand. We reshaped our path to face the direction needed to follow and reach our goals. Let's celebrate women today and let them know they are going to make it after all.

27 "About," Via Travel Service, accessed March 31, 2021.
28 "Jamie Lynn's Story and Training: Meet Jamie Lynn," About us, Wholly Mindful, accessed March 28, 2021.

CHAPTER TWO

The Awesome Women Incubator Model

OUR FEET DIRECT US

After I left Dr. Lert's office, my ankles and feet were too swollen to walk fast. I sat down and looked at my feet, reflecting on their importance. My feet kept me balanced, pointed me in the right direction, and moved me forward to wherever I wanted to head. Over the years prior to, and after, becoming a parent, I met so many women who lost their footing in life. I witnessed how when they got lost and didn't quite know where they were headed, they lifted themselves up, stayed balanced, and continued until they found a viable road.

This book is my gift to women. As women courageously take the road less traveled, I give them a tool to overcome the inevitable obstacles they will face. On their journey, I wish them the ultimate satisfaction of having walked down a path worth their while.

So, face your feet forward. Get your footing in place because we are going on a lifelong journey where you control your future. Ready. Set. Go!

DEVELOPING THE MODEL

I developed this model after speaking with women entrepreneurs for over five years. Some were informal conversations outside the school as we waited for our kids at the end of a school day, others were appointments set up for a tour of my coworking space from women looking to make a change, and others were at events I attended or hosted. As time went on, I observed some clear trends. Namely, I was surrounded by awesome middle-aged women with incredible career potential who lacked professional resources and support. They felt:

- isolated and professionally disconnected.
- incomplete and disappointed with their career progression.
- inadequate about their future earning potential.

For years, I observed when women became business owners, the above was reversed. They achieved personal balance and safety, transforming their mindset to one empowered by future growth. By opening businesses, they exited unwelcoming workplaces and forged a new path for the next generation of women to follow.

As my findings were clarified, I documented similar milestones, emotions, and pain points women experienced as they launched and grew businesses. I placed their experiences into categories and applied key milestones to different tiers of where the business fit in terms of growth. For three years, I tested out the findings and modified them when appropriate.

As I developed my model, a colleague, Jean Roberts-Guequierre, wondered how I could work with a local university who would gladly monitor my progress, the University of Wisconsin Milwaukee's Lubar Entrepreneurship Center (UWM LEC). She connected me to a successful start-up founder, Bob DeVita, one of their team members. He realized the commonality of my work with theirs and immediately invited me to meet with the team.[29] With the encouragement and guidance of the UWM LEC, I officially presented the Awesome Women Incubator Model based on initial interviews with forty-one female business owners from November 27, 2017 to January 26, 2018.

THE IMPACT OF THE AWESOME WOMEN INCUBATOR MODEL

The Awesome Women Incubator Model is important because it gives credence to women business owners common experience. It encapsulates the support needed to navigate each tier of their businesses' growth in line with a woman's mindset. As women business owners assess their point in the model, they gain courage to navigate their path and surpass upcoming milestones, allowing them to set goals and manage expectations at each tier of the model, which could empower more women to scale businesses.

---

29 "Our Community," Lubar Entrepreneurship Center, University of Wisconsin Milwaukee, accessed March 20, 2021.

The model is a talking point for necessary structural change in the areas that hamper the professional growth of women business owners. It places the power into female business owners' capable hands. The model also addresses common roadblocks, including facing fears, accepting realities, building brands, and scaling businesses. Furthermore, the model normalizes the founder's incredibly sensitive emotional state, feelings about financing, and progress with personal branding and needed support at each tier. It is a unique grouping of business owners' development with an elevator pitch, service offering, years in business, networking, and sales development from the idea formation to scaling a business. More information on where you fall can be found on the author page of the MalamaDoe website.[30]

The model gives a roadmap to women who were previously unable to adequately know their future, creating a common understanding and feeling of normalcy across women-owned businesses. When facing the fears which plague most women and accepting a new reality as they travel down this new path, women walk alone. Yet, when they feel isolated, incomplete, and inadequate, as many do in the beginning, they use the information in the model. With this knowledge, they realize their feelings at each leg of the journey are part of a shared experience.

DEFINING THE TIERS OF THE MODEL

The model is divided into a segmentation of six different groups, called tiers, based on where a business owner falls

---

30 "Book by Sheila Long," MalamaDoe, accessed April 7, 2021.

in terms of their business growth. Here is the framework for the tiers where a female business owner may live with a short definition of each, and where they fall in the model.

> **Discovery** occurs when a woman desires to start a business but has not taken any tangible steps toward this goal. This tier is the most challenging to exit, and many never leave it. It takes an emotional toll on those in it and their loved ones.

A good example of a woman in Discovery would be Dr. J.J. Kelly, who sits on the board of a prominent organization in her field of psychology. She is an up-and-coming voice in mental health, yet knows she needs to make a change. J.J. knows her work in the field as a psychologist with troubled teens in a traditional practice is not fulfilling. She cannot imagine doing it much longer. She creates a company and names it UnorthoDocs, Inc.

A woman in this tier craves flexibility. She cannot decide what type of business to open, cannot come up with a name, and cannot determine how her family will survive without her income. She spends countless hours online researching different start-up ideas, networks with others even though she has no plan, and is miserable when thinking about it.

She struggles the most with needing business guidance, navigating flexibility requirements, and calming her internal fears. She needs to:

- reinvent herself to her inner circle and ensure her family will support her prioritizing her career, even at their expense
- determine her funding needs and find flexible employment and emotional support
- select a bank, decide on a business name, and set up a legal entity
- do a self-assessment, using a tool like the "Wheel of Life," and determine a realistic lifestyle with work-life balance

In Discovery, a woman's emotional state is fearful as she is seeking guidance and needs flexibility. Scared to commit and taking baby steps, this woman needs encouragement as she is intimidated and invigorated. She seeks support during this lifestyle change.

If a woman has not started or named her business, yet incessantly talks about it for her entire adult life, she is in Discovery.

Canvasser—An official business owner who has a bank account in her company name which is attached to her legal entity is in the Tier of Canvasser. The founder is actively filling out the Business Model Canvas and proactively working toward getting a paying customer. She owns her future by conducting a thorough self-assessment to achieve balance at work and at home and defines success on her own terms.

Dr. J.J. Kelly decides she must launch a business using Dialectical Behavior Therapy (DBT), which requires treating her kids, or clients, with a foundation of respect. She wants to combine peer coaching and mentorship, while teaching basic coping skills. Her company has been created and named. She is filling out the Business Model Canvas. J.J. begins offering complimentary coaching sessions one day a week on a busy sidewalk in a target neighborhood to gain skills and gather exposure for her business. She spends her down time writing a new book.

If a woman is financially secure, normally because of prior income, loved ones may happily receive this news of her moving forward with a business. However, there is normally disdain for the recent decision because she is not bringing home a paycheck. The entrepreneur is very lonely and is taking baby steps to get her business moving. She needs resources to help her build her company's brand. The biggest pain point is a need for shortcuts to:

- reinvent herself with a new headshot, updated LinkedIn profile, and writing and rehearsing an elevator pitch
- brand her business by getting a business card, deciding on a logo, setting up social media, building a website, and creating marketing plans
- fine-tune her marketing with the appropriate industry-specific terminology, determine her competitive advantage, and get her business in the press
- fulfill initial sales orders and meet with an accountant

In Canvassing, a woman's emotional state is still fearful and scared to commit. She seeks guidance, knowledge, flexibility, and support as this is a solution for work-life balance. If she has experienced betrayal and territorialism, the woman recognizes how it has impeded her progress. She plans a future where success is defined on her own terms.

A woman is in the canvassing tier of the business model for about a year as she determines what works best for the business. This time period could be shorter if she can cut down trial and error from her experience as a business owner where she may have industry connections or money to hire them or understands how key customer demographics make purchasing decisions.

> **Growth**—A business owner who has an accountant, a working website, a social media brand, a streamlined offering, and skin in the game is in the Tier of Growth. She has an operational business with an established brand. This founder is proactively networking and selling, while maintaining a few clients.

Dr. J.J. Kelly publishes her book and rolls it out as a tool for her clients. She promotes her business on social media by conducting live interviews with key thought leaders. She has a few paying clients and is getting booked on podcasts. As she gets exposure in the press, J.J. is thrilled. She realizes initially she will be the one teaching workshops and doing community outreach alongside peer coaching and mentorship, yet she is busy rolling out her business to new and existing clients.

In Growth, a woman's emotional state is quite lonely, and she loves her work. She is all in. She is looking for support as this is a solution for work-life balance. The biggest pain point is the need for an intern as she:

- builds a database to understand the growing lists of people interacting with her business
- creates a social media posting calendar to post and expand her social media, which includes creating business pages and a possible video presence and blog
- seeks funding
- considers reaching out to the press and running ads

If a woman has strangers recognizing her business logo and has recently begun earning money from paying clients, yet is constantly proactively marketing her business, she is in Growth. A woman can be in Growth for one to four years, depending on how the market is faring and the financial and time investment she puts into her business.

Prospering—A business owner who has taken on debt and is viewed as running a business which will be around for a while is in the Tier of Prospering. She has sales coming in for the business, with 40 percent being reactive and 60 percent proactive. She needs to hire staff and her time is precious.

Dr J.J. Kelly has rolled out her YouTube Channel, is a sought-out speaker on the social media app ClubHouse, and is expanding her service to a few local learning institutions to use her insights in classrooms. Her groundbreaking idea of teaching basic coping skills and emotion regulation as mainstream teachings is gaining traction. She has full days of meetings with paying clients. She has hired staff and can adequately pay them.

In Prospering, a woman can embrace happiness. She is stressed and under pressure, and she is looking to improve the quality of work, which may require revisiting her business plan. She is looking for support as she reevaluates and prioritizes what she is juggling personally and professionally. The biggest pain point is hiring staff, specifically interns and sales help, as she:

- wins awards
- attends trade shows
- enters the speaker circuit
- seeks funding through microlending or investor pitching

If a woman has no free time and does not want to have lunch or coffee or network with anyone because she has not yet hired staff to adequately help her yet is in constant contact with reacting to the needs of paying customers and dedicated to their satisfaction, she is in Prosperer.

A woman business owner typically prospers approximately five years after opening. She may arrive sooner if she is not a first-time business owner, has valuable connections, or sells a hugely successful item. If she has not devoted adequate time or resources to her business, she may not get to this point or it may take longer.

> **Fulfillment**—A woman business owner who has successfully run a business and is viewed as a leader in the community is in the Tier of Fulfillment. A woman is not just a business owner, but a Brand. She keeps her staff to a manageable amount, fewer than five employees, and gives back to pet causes

in the community with her voice and donations. The owner has low concerns and a memorized elevator pitch. She has "made it."

J.J. Kelly's book is being sold in local stores and she is a sought-after speaker. Her business, UnorthoDocs, Inc., has its content and peer coaching ideas used in many educational institutions throughout her region. She is well established as a leader in the DBT Field and appreciated for her efforts. J.J. gives back to the community by sitting on the boards of the Self-Harm Crisis Text Line, offers her services pro-bono to needed organizations, and speaks at many local conferences.

A woman who does not pursue any more business best depict this tier. She stops answering emails from ideal partners who want to help elevate her business. She may hire a few staff people to help with order fulfillment and keep the business manageable at a single fulfillment location.

In Fulfillment, a woman achieves an abundant mindset. She is in pursuit of happiness and has hit a personal sweet spot. She looks at her business from the big picture. She seeks support while reevaluating and prioritizing what she is juggling personally and professionally. She seeks to:

- hire trustworthy staff
- fund her business
- fine-tune her messaging

If a woman has extra income and time to spend on causes near and dear to her heart, which are not related to volunteering for her children, yet is a small business owner with fewer than five employees, she is in Fulfillment.

A woman is in this tier after ten-plus years in business and probably will be in it until she retires.

> **Expansion**—A woman business owner who has decided that she will not just settle with a business that found success instead uses her Brand to assist her as she wants to continue expanding. This woman could be an accomplished author, a successful speaker, or an award winner seeking to expand her service offering. She is comfortable with change and aims to continue to expand.

Dr. J.J. Kelly works with national mental health organizations and leading parenting groups to ensure that all kids have coping skills in high school. She aims to have her UnorthoDocs, Inc., teachings implemented as a mandatory course in all high schools across the country.

The founder now inspires others through speaking engagements to give back in meaningful ways and donates a part of her profits to charity. If a woman does not think twice about taking on debt to open a new location for her business, or expand in a new arena, and is excited to take on a new opportunity, she is in Expansion.

In Expansion, a woman's emotional state is nervous, thrilled, and optimistic. She is looking for support as she reevaluates and prioritizes what she is juggling personally and professionally. She has no pain point and seeks to hire capable staff.

A woman is in this tier after over seven years in business and may stay until retirement.

To summarize, the customer tiers of Discovery, Canvasser, Growth, Prosperer, Fulfillment, and Expansion are all important and represent different tiers and trends of where a founder is with her business.

One awesome woman who is doing her part to help others succeed is Jane Finette.

CREATING OUR COMPANY

Jane Finette runs The Coaching Fellowship, which specializes in leadership coaching for young women social change leaders. Jane ensures these women, who are in the "impact space," work in a job tied closely to their values. She explains:

"If you can ignite what a woman really cares about, what she's doing, why she's putting in the time, you will find this fierce woman who's willing to step forward. If we can pull out of someone—What really matters? What are you? What do you stand for? What is your stake? What are you here in this lifetime to do? They will take risks and be willing to step up to the leadership."

To get more women to this point, we need to better understand the path we have traveled. Let's review the two types of companies whose practices cause women to start businesses. They are explained in relation to the model here.

In an **exclusive company** which has not evolved since the 1970s, its structure was set up without regard for women, thus the odds are stacked against women who are challenged to thrive. The company's current leadership sees no need to address any inequity and be more friendly to women, and thus makes no effort to evolve. An example of this is a company which has been operational for over forty years and does not have working policies in place to proactively address sexual harassment and follow up on out-of-the-ordinary personal leave requests.

In an **evolving company**, its culture caters to, and promotes, a certain gender, race, background, or personality type. Normally, a woman does not easily fit in, yet the company is making an effort to address the inequity previously mentioned. As it makes amends, the existing staff who also feel misaligned may experience backdraft as the inequity is addressed. This occurrence of backdraft is described by mindful self-compassion expert Kristin Neff as "when we give ourselves unconditional love, we discover the conditions under which we were unloved."[31]

---

31   Dr. Kristen Neff, "Tips for Practice," Practices, Self-Compassion, accessed February 13, 2021.

In the **inclusive company,** represented in the Awesome Women Incubator Model, a woman expects self-respect and may acknowledge she does not belong in an exclusive or evolving company. She now faces the repercussions of hiding her authentic self to survive in such an environment. The entrepreneur experiences a sense of betrayal.

"Betrayal is not something we want to experience, because it brings with it all the fear, anger, sadness, and shame. Betrayal can feel like failure, if we view it only through the eyes of traditional models of leadership. But betrayal is also a pivotal moment of choice, where the breaking point is suddenly obvious, and our decision becomes clear. Betrayal is imperative because it shatters our illusions and takes us down the Heroine's Journey path to transformation."

ELIZABETH MCLAUGHLIN[32]

---

32   Elizabeth McLaughlin, "The Heroine's Journey: Betrayal," Gaia Leadership Project, accessed February 8, 2021.

The betrayal can be professional, but it can also be personal and is discussed in more depth in Chapter Five.

By using the **Awesome Women Incubator Model**, one clearly understands the common attributes encountered as the idea grows into a viable, and scalable, business. It measures success with manageable deliverables that account for the varying emotional state and feelings about funding which become more predictable as the business grows. The model validates the company's progress, meeting goals and expectations as it reaches each new tier.

The relationship with the tiers impacts a woman's psyche as she moves forward to create and grow a business. For example, when she contemplates opening a business and plans out how it will look, she may work in, or have recently exited, an environment with an exclusive or evolving company. Yet, as she builds her company, she creates a culture where she belongs.

A woman is normally working at an exclusive or evolving company in the first two tiers, **Discovery** and **Canvasser,** while laying the groundwork for her company. As she builds her business, she fully enters the Awesome Women Model and evolves into the tiers of **Growth, Prosperer, Fulfillment,** and **Expansion**. Since the relationship with existing companies is so intertwined with the first two Tiers and not so much with the latter four, I break out Discovery and Canvasser below.

In **Discovery**, a woman enters this Tier for one of two reasons. She works for an outdated or evolving company that is not a good fit, or she is in a personal situation where she needs to make a change and wants to be her own boss for reasons which may, or may not, be related to a personal or professional betrayal. Regardless, she seeks guidance and needs resources. She is quite fearful and desperately needs some flexibility.

In **Canvasser,** a woman sets up the framework for her business with a business model canvas, which is discussed more in Chapter Six. She simultaneously works on a self-assessment, such as the Wheel of Life, to evaluate what truly works for her. She lays the groundwork for her business to best position it on solid footing.

To successfully move forward along the tiers of the Awesome Women model, women must determine what works by going through a self-assessment. The groundwork for this is laid during **Discovery** and the self-assessment work is done during the tier of **Canvasser.** Be it through mindfulness, faith, or past experience, a woman acknowledges her strong feelings and realizes her values through it. To move forward with our goal, a woman determines which path we can, and cannot, move down.

During the self-assessment, a business owner creates and evaluates her Wheel of Life and Business Model Canvas, which are discussed in Chapter Three and Six. A woman has the flexibility, free from the time restrictions of a manager, and benefits immensely. One such way is assessing her feelings about her finances.

WOMEN AND FINANCIAL GUILT

When contemplating a business, a woman business owner experiences strong feelings of fear and financial guilt. It is critical she use a tool such as the Wheel of Life to do a self-assessment to evaluate the power and network dynamics at play in her life. She must then move forward onto a viable path while becoming a business owner.

A woman in **Discovery** may have major financial guilt. Ashamed, as she knows she needs to support others financially, she wants to follow her dreams, which may place providing for others in jeopardy. It pains her tremendously.

Two surveys by SCORE and Goldman Sachs on how businesses are funded provide credence to how women, who care for their family, bear the heavy weight of not growing our money, but taking it out of personal savings to grow a business and our dream. Instead of a nice vacation, a shopping spree for new clothes, or to attend a fun summer camp, we either forgo these luxuries or put the expenditures on a credit card. We know that instead of building value in our home or retirement, we may need to take out a home equity line of credit. This is a hard pill to swallow for women.[33][34]

Worse yet, the other type of financing is that of private investments of family and friends. When a woman is viewed as one who keeps the family together, yet wants to pursue her dreams,

---

33 "The Megaphone of Main Street: Women's Entrepreneurship, Infographic #4: How and Why Women Start Businesses," Score, November 5, 2018, accessed March 27, 2021.

34 Goldman Sachs, *Voice of Small Business in America: 2019 Insights Report* (New York: Goldman Sachs, 2019), 31.

those "donating" to her cause may be also passing judgment on the impact of the decision on other family members.[35]

When it came time for me to open my business, I was a few weeks away from finalizing my funding and signing the lease required a down payment. A friend came forward as an investor with a short-term loan. I had to do my own self-assessment about finances, risk, and respect. I moved forward, taking and then promptly paying back her loan, which worked for me personally and professionally.

Research has shown women and men assess the risk of taking on responsibility differently. This is discussed in further detail in Chapter Eleven. Here is a great example of how a manager understands and works with the parameters of differing priorities.

THE IMPORTANCE OF CERTAINTY IN A SELF-ASSESSMENT

Dave Vasko is a director of research and development at an evolving large multinational technology company called Rockwell Automation. He wants to make Rockwell more inclusive for women and BIPOC communities. Dave is entrusted with hiring more women and is saddened when leaders at diversity conferences see no repercussions to their lack of representation.

Dave realizes things are changing in terms of workplace flexibility. As companies and coworkers understand the need

---

35   Ibid.

for personal wellbeing and the importance of balancing it to have a productive employee in the long run, "setting priorities and not feeling guilty about it" becomes the norm, and it impacts both women and men at home. He remembers when Rockwell implemented a summer schedule of a 4.5-day work week: "Until the people at the top started using it, it was not being used by the employees."

However, when dealing with women versus men, Dave uses "calibration." In his experience, he is aware of research indicating that women sometimes undersell their experience and capabilities at work, and he wants to be part of the solution. "We all need to be able to bring our entire selves to work. That's really important."

Dave witnessed how some women may not attempt to take on additional responsibilities and recognizes they may need more information about the true requirements before fully "committing" to a task. Communication and regular check-ups are important to understand the problems people are facing. He recalled, "Some of my best performance appraisals have been whether they've had a really big glaring problem. We've talked about it, and it almost invariably addresses something holding them back."

Dave is part of a company which is taking the strides to support women, and he sees what is important in this new era. As we work toward defining our parameters in our own business, we must see the importance of our own actions to establish good relationships, value our flexibility, and ensure we are certain about the choices we will take on so we can achieve the needed balance in our life.

NEXT STEPS

Now that the tiers of the Awesome Women Incubator Model are defined, a business owner can decide where they fall on the journey. They know how to remain satisfied business owners moving down the path that works best for them. They want to run a business where they belong.

To succeed here, they need to:

- Accept they are in the path of recovery from Betrayal while starting a new, exhilarating adventure as a business owner during the tiers of Discovery and Canvasser
- Realize where they fall on a self-assessment
- Celebrate their risk-alert tactics and social sensitivity, allowing for incredible collaboration
- Create a path to follow as business owners

By taking these critical steps and recognizing trends that create empowered women, they will learn what works best for them and set themselves up for a future where they can thrive. Women have the potential to drastically change the landscape for women, and by owning their own future, they can make an impact as Malala Yousafzai challenged us at the 2013 Youth Takeover of the United Nations.

"We cannot all succeed when half of us are held back. We call upon our sisters around the world to be brave—to embrace

the strength within themselves and realize
their full potential."[36]

A single decision can transform a life.

---

36 "Malala Yousafzai's Speech at the Youth Takeover of the United Nations,"
    Explainers (blog), *Their World*, July 12, 2013, accessed February 8, 2021.

CHAPTER THREE

The Inspiring Opportunity Entrepreneur

———

STARTING AND GROWING UNORTHODOCS

"How about we shoot a little higher, toward joy instead of just existing?" This quote is on Dr. J.J. Kelly, PysD, a San Francisco Bay psychologist's, Facebook page. It depicts how she has lived her life.[37] J.J.'s outgoing style and willingness to stand up for what is right has been apparent since we were childhood friends. She aims to make change where necessary, and as a psychologist, she treats her "teenagers and young adults with a foundation of respect." As we saw in Chapter Two with J.J.'s example, she has moved around many of the different tiers of the Awesome Women model.

As entrepreneurship is an overriding topic which can overwhelm, I find there to be an overlap in the difference between

---

37   J.J. Kelly, "How about we shoot a little higher, toward joy instead of just existing?," Facebook, January 9, 2021.

what is a small business owner versus what is an entrepreneur. From my viewpoint, someone who starts a business is an entrepreneur and they become a small business owner, ideally when they settle into the Tier of Fulfillment. Over time, the founder ceases to look at themselves as an entrepreneur and finds the description of a small business owner to be more fitting.

Dr. J.J. Kelly walked the path of becoming a small business owner when she began working as a licensed psychologist after successfully interning for a prestigious forward-thinking center in liberal Berkeley, California. She was offered and accepted a staff position working there. Dr. Kelly successfully grew her business, ran group sessions and established a successful practice taking in troubled teenager clients. She became one of the up-and-coming voices in mental health.

Yet, J.J. realized she was working in a broken industry, and in late 2019, she "gave up a lucrative private practice in favor of a movement." Dr. Kelly founded UnorthoDocs, Inc., where advanced students are elevated to "docs" as peer-coaches.[38] She knew that to truly impact change, she must educate on new techniques with workshops, community outreach, peer coaching and mentorship. J.J. aims to scale her business by having her insights taught in learning institutions, with core sessions such as basic coping skills and emotional regulation used as mainstream teachings. Nowadays, J.J.'s Facebook banner depicts her values. It reads, "The writing's on the wall."

---

38   J.J. Kelly, "About J.J.," Dr. J.J. Kelly, accessed March 31, 2021.

J.J. is the author of *Holy Sh*t, My Kid Is Cutting: The Complete Plan to Stop Self Harm*, which she wrote as a parenting manual.[39] She also wrote *Holy Shit, I'm A Gifted "Misfit"!: The Young Folx Guide to Unlock Your Superpowers*, which is meant to be a tool for her clients.[40]

J.J.'s story is a great example of what it looks like to start a business as a necessity entrepreneur and reach the Tier of Fulfillment, but not want to continue in the Tier of Expansion because of an internal conflict. She exemplifies what happens when a business owner reassesses their established businesses goals and starts over. Even after starting a new business, Dr. Kelly was positioned for success because she built a successful brand as a leading psychologist. She could launch and scale UnorthoDocs easily, and as she trained others to face their fears, she had the skills to help navigate her own. Yet, when J.J. started over as an opportunity entrepreneur, she still experienced the normal fears typical of a necessity entrepreneur. While navigating this financial instability, J.J. has the background, determination, and knowledge to scale her business, transforming lives in the process.

TYPES OF ENTREPRENEURS

Women starting businesses is a large trend. A 2020 article entitled "Twenty-Two Mind-Blowing Women Entrepreneur Statistics" states, "In the last twenty years, the number of

39 J. J. Kelly PsyD., *Holy Sh*t, My Kid Is Cutting: The Complete Plan to Stop Self Harm* (Washington D.C.: Difference Press, 2020).

40 J. J. Kelly PsyD., *Holy Shit, I'm A Gifted "Misfit"!: The Young Folx Guide to Unlock Your Superpowers* (Oakland: Independently published, 2020).

businesses owned by women in the US has increased by 114%." Also, nearly two-thirds of female founders are in their forties or fifties and over four-fifths have college degrees.[41] Women-led business employment has increased by 8 percent, more than the 1.8 percent for all businesses.[42] To best explain these numbers, we need to understand exactly who the statistics represent and what they do. There are different types of entrepreneurs:

- Necessity
- Flexibility
- Sideprenuer
- Opportunity

Each career stage has different objectives. First of all, there is the Necessity Entrepreneur who starts a business after being terminated from a job. They account for over 28 percent of Baby Boomers.[43]

A **Necessity Entrepreneur** is an individual who "cannot find quality employment or is unemployed. Their only viable employment option is to

---

41 Branka Vuleta, "22 Mind-Blowing Women Entrepreneurs Statistics," *What To Become* (blog), August, 11, 2020.

42 American Express, *The 2019 State of Women-Owned Business Report* (New York: American Express, 2019), 3.

43 "The Megaphone of Main Street: Women's Entrepreneurship, Infographic #4: How and Why Women Start Businesses," Score, November 5, 2018.

start a business. This definition also includes women who, though employed, need to supplement their income."[44]

Then there is the Flexibility Entrepreneur.

A **Flexibility Entrepreneur** requires time and place flexibility "because workforce policies do not accommodate their caregiving responsibilities, or they desire more control over when and where they work."[45]

I know many Flexibility and Necessity Entrepreneurs. According to SCORE, a group which assists in the start-up ecosystem, they found that nearly 26 percent "of Generation Xers stated family consideration" as their driving force for founding a business.[46]

They need a job and cannot find one that fits in with their additional responsibilities, especially caretaking.

---

44 American Express, *The 2019 State of Women-Owned Business Report*, 4.
45 Ibid.
46 "The Megaphone of Main Street: Women's Entrepreneurship, Infographic #4: How and Why Women Start Businesses," Score, November 5, 2018.

Sometimes women will become employed on the side working a few hours, which leads us to our next definition of the Sidepreneur.

A **Sidepreneur** consists of a business owner "testing a business idea while holding down a job, or supplementing income, or seeing a creative outlet or additional challenge. They may also want flexibility because they have caregiving responsibilities or want a certain lifestyle."[47]

Women entrepreneurs in the flexibility, necessity, and sidepreneur career stages are not primarily focused on hiring employees or growing revenue excessively. They simply focus on value-based progress, which is elaborated on in future chapters. The focus is different for our final entrepreneur type, the Opportunity Entrepreneur.

"An **Opportunity Entrepreneur** sees possibilities in the market that they want

---

47 American Express, *The 2019 State of Women-Owned Business Report*, 2.

to exploit. They are more likely to enter the market in good economic times than in bad. These businesses have a higher rate of survival and better growth prospects than their necessity and flexibility counterparts. During good economic times, opportunity entrepreneurship rises."[48]

On my entrepreneurship and lifelong journey, I have been surrounded by women who were in the Flexibility, Necessity and Sidepreneur stages of their career. As their business grows and thrives, they may move into the category of the Opportunity Entrepreneur.

I appreciate and celebrate the Opportunity Entrepreneur. They are the leaders of today and tomorrow. They stand up for women in the necessity and flexibility career stage. I hear them speak at women-focused events, letting everyone in the room know that they succeed because of the support that they have in the home. Their voices need to be heard.

The Opportunity Entrepreneur has the ultimate job fit. In my daily experience with suburban women who work in entrepreneurship, we all aspire to be like the few Opportunity Entrepreneurs we know. They are their own boss and work on growing a business that will change the world. As their

---

48   Ibid.

business expands into multiple fields, they become bigger than their company; they become a Brand.

Three of these women are my friends and colleagues Amanda Baltz, Sr. Kathleen Long, and Anne Machesky. Here are their inspiring stories.

AMANDA BALTZ TEACHES COMPASSION

Amanda Baltz, who we heard about in the Introduction, started out as a Flexibility Entrepreneur. She was working full time as a pharmaceutical rep and was a pregnant mother with a toddler seeking work-life balance. Amanda left that role to help build an amazing company, Spaulding Clinical.[49] It was a great match for her background with a major in biomedical science, interest in medical school, and working as a pharmaceutical rep. About a year into the venture, the 2008 recession hit. Then, she learned that her initial idea of having more flexibility and better work-life balance in her career would not be the case.

She was put in charge of the day-to-day operations of the company dealing with vendor, bank, and real estate concerns and received her self-proclaimed MBA of "Baptism by Fire." As she learned the ins and outs of business, she "fell in love" with it because, while her dad was "pitching for capital," she was rolling out the strategy on the back end. The business had grown from zero to 15 million dollars of revenue in 2012 when Amanda and her father came into our children's school to speak for "Career Day."

---

49 "Home," Spaulding Clinical, accessed March 31, 2021.

They sold a product which could wirelessly monitor the heartbeat from a computer with the key information being stored on the cloud, thus being able to be easily accessed for patients who could not make it to the doctor. That day at school, my children witnessed its functionality and came home talking about how cool this product was that their classmate's family created. The coolest part was how a classmate, Amanda's son, was able to remove his shirt in school to attach the product to his heart. Over time, this revolutionary new product become an instrumental tool to monitor cardiac health.

SR. KATHLEEN TEACHES SOCIAL JUSTICE

Sometimes, you don't have to own a business to be an opportunity entrepreneur. There are less traditional routes to follow which can lead to amazing outcomes, and the spirit of entrepreneurship can prevail. One such person is Sr. Kathleen Long, who worked as a social worker in fragile, start-up organizations and made them work with her tenacity, skills, enjoyment, and values. While being the boss, she made the decisions and enriched the lives around her with her vision. She was recently honored by the Archdiocese of Chicago with the "St. Teresa of Avila Award, given in recognition of a woman religious or order in Hispanic Ministry."[50]

When I was a child, my aunt became ordained a Catholic Sister in the Order of Preachers (O.P.). She was very involved in the fight for social justice, including taking opportunities working at an orphanage in Bolivia, running a parish center

---

50   Archdiocese of Chicago, "Archdiocese of Chicago Celebrates 18th Annual Noche de Gala with Theme 'Celebrating the Extraordinary Jubilee of Mercy'," news release, September 27, 2016, accessed January 18, 2020.

in a Latinx immigrant neighborhood, and attending protests to fight for the rights of all the forgotten.

She joined the fight to close the School of the Americas, a US federal military operation which trained foreign organizations on torture techniques. To raise awareness, Kathleen defied police orders after crossing a makeshift line. She was held for three months in a US federal prison.[51]

Upon her release, she received a job offer to run a social justice retreat center in Cuernavaca, Mexico, where visiting college students from Canada and the United States would be inspired by her story. Kathleen grew this organization with retention and by creating service opportunities for them to improve the living conditions of local townspeople. Kathleen's actions inspired nearly one thousand retreat attendees.[52]

In an interview with the Global Sisters Project, Sr. Kathleen Long shows how she lives for others: "They all want truth and justice, they want a good job, they want to take care of their kids, they want to take care of their health care needs, they want to contribute to society. That's what energizes me, walking with people to make those changes."[53]

51 Jeff Kurowski, "Appleton Nun Arrested in Protest," *The Compass*, December 6, 2002, accessed January 18, 2021.

52 Soli Salgado, "Q&A with Sr. Kathleen Long, Helping Immigrants Become U.S. Citizens," *Global Sisters Report* (blog), September 28, 2016, accessed March 31, 2021.

53 Ibid.

ANNE MACHESKY ACCOUNTS FOR WOMEN'S FINANCIAL PLANS

Through my work, I have had the great honor of meeting many wonderful people. One such person is Anne Machesky. I view Anne as an Opportunity Entrepreneur because, in 1980, she entered a new field, called financial planning, which customers viewed as a cross between a stockbroker, estate lawyer, and insurance agent. Anne chose this field not out of necessity, but purely for the love of helping others. She loved the incredible opportunity to create her own identity alongside the newfound ideas of investments, while educating clients what those investments would do and could be. She was drawn to the planning and helping others in the process. Originally, she worked primarily in corporate financial planning seminars where normally the only women in the room worked in human resources and set up the meeting but did not attend.

Anne started in her field in 1980 and "the backdrop was clearly white married men." She realized that when helping couples with financial advice, men were more outspoken and women "weren't either given a chance to, or didn't, assert their voice as far as their future, their values." She realized from the beginning that "women were very unprepared financially, because most of the monetary funnel, meaning pensions and such, came from the man's job."

Anne noted that as female advisors entered the field, they paid more attention to women clients, seeing that their goals would be set, which included the goals of the family. She recalls, "the more women asserted their voices, not just about money, but also about value, their jobs and what it meant to them. That started to change the dynamic in conversations."

Anne remembered how it was hard for married men to adjust. Early in her career, Anne had one experience meeting with a married couple. When Anne asked about the family financial and future goals, the wife began to answer but her husband raised his hand up basically saying, "Don't talk. Stop!"

Anne respectfully conducted the meeting, but afterward turned them down as a client. Her reasoning was based on how the husband's behavior was unacceptable.

"His wife had a voice, she had values, and he wasn't willing to even bring them into the room. So that was not going to help the couple succeed in planning for their future as both individual's needs must be part of the planning and it wasn't gonna work for me, when he wanted to muzzle anyone in the business relationship."

Anne grew up in a home where her father treated her mother with respect, and she was appalled by how this man treated his wife. She could not accept this treatment. It went against her principles. It also goes against those of this chapter. Women belong at the table, they have skills, and they should be able to grow in a world without fear of repercussions.

ANNE'S NEW EYES ON NWYZE

Nowadays, Anne is a well-respected leader in her field. Because of her incredible success and mindset in the industry of insurance and financial services, she was featured in the 2015 book entitled *Financial Services: Women at the Top: A Woman in Insurance and Financial Services Research Study.*[54]

Anne has many talents that position opportunity for individuals and business through disrupting, reframing, and rebuilding their thinking about their life challenges. As a gifted poet, Anne has used her poetic vision to lead while creating an avenue to getting to the heart of the matter. Her visionary communication and problem-solving skills have been featured at large meetings and conferences, including the National Women in Financial Services Conference in 2019.

Anne has recently relaunched her consulting company called Nwyze, which offers "a new way to expand your eyes, open your thinking, and change your perspective to empower and guide you in your transformational journey through: *Keynotes, Workshops, Mastery Classes, and Coaching.*"[55]

PURSUING OUTSTANDING OPPORTUNITIES

Opportunity Entrepreneurs are our aspiration and inspiration. We must remember that they normally do not start out with an incredible idea. They begin for different reasons that best meet their lifestyle.

---

54 Athea Reed and Diane Dixon, *Financial Services: Women at the Top: A Women in Insurance and Financial Services Research Study* (Indiana: iUniverse, July 31, 2015).

55 "Home Page," Nwyze, accessed March 29, 2021.

- J.J. Kelly built her practice as a Necessity Entrepreneur and eventually migrated to one of an Opportunity Entrepreneur when she had a better feel for the market and its shortcomings. She was well established by that point.
- Amanda Baltz began as a Flexibility Entrepreneur, and with the shift in market demands, she lost the flexibility she initially sought. She eventually became an Opportunity Entrepreneur when she spun off her own company.
- Sr. Kathleen Long started out seeking peace and justice for the underrepresented as a Sidepreneur, doing what she could to improve in her daily role and cherishing her role as a peacemaker.
- Anne Machesky began as a Necessity Entrepreneur, knowing the career potential of venturing down this unchartered territory could lead her down the path of the Opportunity Entrepreneur. She has helped and inspired countless men, women, and families.

Let's work on helping the future Opportunity Entrepreneurs arrive by being open and vulnerable to the fear women face. As they take on new ventures and additional financial risks to use their skills differently, let's celebrate these pioneers for navigating uncharted territories. They are the Opportunity Entrepreneurs and are guides for the next generation of women as they pass through uncharted territories.

They walk their own path, follow their own star, and they have their own values which drive the decisions to run their businesses. They take it one day at a time.

PART TWO

BREAKING AWAY

CHAPTER FOUR

The Birth of Necessity and Flexibility Entrepreneurs

———

THE IRONY OF PHYLLIS SCHLAFLY'S CRUSADE

"Stop Taking Our Privileges -Equal Rights Amendment!"
Phyllis Schlafly carried her sign with the name of her well-known organization STOP ERA, aiming to derail legislation giving equal rights to women. She was known to thrill audiences of mobilized churchgoers of all faiths, be they Mormon, Jewish, Protestant, or Catholic. As her supporters cheered on Phyllis, they did not see the hypocrisy of it all. She ran for office multiple times over fourteen years while bearing six children. Yet, they listened as this highly educated, financially privileged would-be-elected official had caretakers watching her babies at home.

Although Phyllis' career underscored her life as a liberated woman, her followers who lacked the same resources and support listened as she lectured them to take necessary steps to help her ruin women's chances at workplace equity by ensuring they did not gain equal rights and stayed in their roles, ideally as a homemaker. The irony was apparent. Phyllis was not a homemaker. To further Phyllis' cause, they volunteered at STOP ERA.[56]

"In the 1970s, Mrs. Schlafly's campaign against the Equal Rights Amendment played a large part in its undoing. The amendment would have expanded women's rights by barring any gender-based distinctions in federal and state laws, and it was within hailing distance of becoming the law of the land."

DOUGLAS MARTIN, *NEW YORK TIMES* [57]

Phyllis was one of the privileged few for whom paying for childcare was not an issue. Phyllis married an older, wealthy man who increased her standard of living substantially. With

---

56   Lesley Kennedy, "How Phyllis Schlafly Derailed the Equal Rights Amendment," *History.com*, March 19, 2020, accessed February 9, 2021.

57   Douglas Martin, "Phyllis Schlafly, 'First Lady' of a Political March to the Right, Dies at 92," *New York Times*, September 6, 2016, accessed February 9, 2021.

her balanced lifestyle where she received financial, emotional, household, and professional support, she then proclaimed high moral standards and launched a business where she was fulfilled professionally with the mission being that the privileged place in society was being a homemaker. She knew women desperately lacked the support she had. Yet, with her finances and subsequent support, she created and led a crusade to stop the creation of a more equitable future for women throughout the United States.

As she continued to derail the rights of those without adequate support, she became known nationally for her beliefs opposing equal rights for women. She had many books written about her, one with the fitting name: *Phyllis Schlafly; the Sweetheart of the Silent Majority*.[58] [59] She authored many books, including *The Power of the Positive Woman*, which gave arguments against radical feminism by discussing her life as a Christian and mother.[60] [61]

"(Phyllis) wrote or edited more than twenty books, published an influential

58 Eileen Jones, "There's Nothing Good about Phyllis Schlafly," *Jacobin Mag*, May 20, 2020.

59 Carol Felsenthal, *Phyllis Schlafly; The Sweetheart of the Silent Majority* (Washington D.C.: Regnery Gateway, January 1, 1982).

60 Phyllis Schlafly, *The Power of the Positive Woman* (New York City: Crown Pub, July 1, 1977).

61 Douglas Martin, "Phyllis Schlafly, 'First Lady' of a Political March to the Right, Dies at 92," *New York Times*, September 6, 2016, accessed February 9, 2021.

monthly newsletter beginning in 1967,
appeared daily on nearly 500 radio stations
and delivered regular commentaries
on CBS television in the 1970s and
CNN in the eighties."

DOUGLAS MARTIN, *NEW YORK TIMES* [62]

After creating STOP ERA, to more voraciously argue against equality for her gender, Phyllis again used her resources to become a lawyer.[63] Her efforts as a woman who had financial, emotional, household, and professional support successfully derailed the Equal Rights Amendment fighting for the rights of those who lacked support.

"Both houses of Congress had passed it by
a vote of more than 90 percent, and thirty-five state legislatures — only three shy of
the number required for adoption — had
approved it. But the amendment lost steam
in the late 1970s under pressure from Mrs.
Schlafly's volunteer brigades. Despite an

---

62   Ibid.
63   Ibid.

extension of the deadline, the amendment died, on June 30, 1982."

DOUGLAS MARTIN, *NEW YORK TIMES* [64]

The unparalleled damage Phyllis did to the prospects of other struggling would-be businesswomen are felt to this day. She is a woman who had balanced support yet had no empathy for less fortunate women who did not. Phyllis is featured in the 2020 nine-episode series on Hulu and FX called *Mrs. America*. Her "monstrous" impact of spreading "dangerous and hateful" attitudes was felt by many, from the homosexuals who she felt deserved no rights, to sexual abuse survivors who she blamed as not being "virtuous."[65] [66]

The result of Phyllis' actions caused the many financial, emotional, household, and professional support inequities women face today with the unfortunate repercussions outlined throughout the remaining chapters of this book. One major area where the impact of the failure of the Equal Rights Amendment being passed was felt was on caretakers.

---

64 Ibid.

65 Eileen Jones, "There's Nothing Good about Phyllis Schlafly," *Jacobin Mag*, May 20, 2020.

66 Douglas Martin, "Phyllis Schlafly, 'First Lady' of a Political March to the Right, Dies at 92," *New York Times*, September 6, 2016, accessed February 9, 2021.

HOW A SUPPORTIVE FELLOW CARETAKER CHANGED MY CAREER TRAJECTORY

"I just don't have anyone to watch my kids. I have tried everyone I normally ask, and I don't have a babysitter who is available." I sat across from my friend, colleague, and fellow school parent Jamie Lynn Tatera as we took a break from swapping our consulting services for each other. She had been coaching me on mindful self-compassion while I refined the service she would offer for her soon-to-launch business, Wholly Mindful.[67] I was attempting to fully exit my seemingly endless stay in the Tier of Discovery.

I looked over at our children playing together nearby and continued, "I was invited to an incredible networking dinner and already planned to attend the conference the next day. It could be the key to getting my career back on track, but it is out of town. To attend, I will need to be gone for a day and a half."

Jamie Lynn knew my kids and saw how I was in a tough spot. She knew that, because of my caretaking responsibilities, I was on track to entering the career stage of a Flexibility Entrepreneur. The next day she called me saying, "I have thought it over and I will watch your kids for the needed hours. Our kids will have a blast together. You need to go to this event."

Floored, elated, and eternally grateful, Jamie Lynn provided some much-needed, trusted childcare so I could gain fresh input and attend my alma mater's Fifth Annual Booth Women Connect conference. This year's topic was

---

67   "Jamie Lynn's Story and Training: Meet Jamie Lynn," About us, Wholly Mindful, accessed March 28, 2021.

very pertinent to me, it was a rally call for more women to return to the workplace.[68]

I attended the dinner they had invited me to the night before and made some great contacts while having a wonderful evening. The next day, in a keynote address, our popular, outspoken entrepreneurship professor at the University of Chicago Booth School of Business, Waverly Deutsch, spoke about "Women in Entrepreneurship: The Story Behind the Data."[69] She brought up a controversial topic in homes with small children—caretaking. She challenged us to become the primary breadwinner in the home, letting us know, "If you are not married to a man who is 'man enough' to step back in his career, then get some help in the home." She demanded we pay our caretakers well, treat them as a member of our family, and see the importance of raising a child. Because in the end this is all that really matters: raising a child with caring, supportive adults.

Then, she vehemently demanded to the women business leaders sitting in front of her that we pursue our goals, dream big, and create amazing businesses that are outside of the box and in industries where women are not prevalent. She then gave the audience the following objectives:

1. Be Bold
2. Learn How to Sell

68 University of Chicago Booth School of Business, "Booth Women Connect 2015, Women in Entrepreneurship: The Story Behind the Data, Professor Waverly Deutsch," Facebook, November 11, 2015, accessed March 28, 2021.

69 Waverly Deutsch, "Women in Entrepreneurship: The Story Behind the Data" (Powerpoint presentation, 5th Annual Booth Women Connect Conference, The University of Chicago Booth School of Business Booth Women Connect, Chicago, IL, October 23, 2015).

3. Ask.
4. Pay It Forward
5. Think Big[70] [71]

I left the conference inspired by her rally call and wishing I could be on board. Yet, I knew getting help in the home would be a struggle, as it would be for many others in my neighborhood. I remembered a self-assessment tool I had been introduced to by my executive business coach, Elene Cafasso, with Enerpace, Inc., called the Wheel of Life. It was time for a quick self- assessment with this easy-to-apply tool which allowed me to implement quick change.[72]

CREATING A BALANCED WHEEL OF LIFE WITH A SELF-ASSESSMENT

There are many ways to evaluate yourself. In the traditional workplace with a manager, there are the annual reviews that come with an evaluation on how you compare based on what that the company needs and how you fit. Yet, when you set up your own company, you need to determine what works best for you. You want to position yourself for success.

I recommend using the tool I had just referenced, the Wheel of Life, because it shows how our personal, professional, and emotional worlds are interconnected.

---

70   Ibid.

71   University of Chicago Booth School of Business, "Booth Women Connect 2015, Women in Entrepreneurship: The Story Behind the Data, Professor Waverly Deutsch," Facebook, November 11,2015, accessed March 28, 2021.

72   Elene Cafasso, "A Balanced Life: What Is It?," *Enerpace, Inc.* (blog), December 2, 2020, accessed February 8, 2021.

Wheel of Life

Career

Friends and Family

Fun and Recreation

Health

Money

Personal Growth

Physical Environment

Significant Other

Elene explains how to use it in her blog, "A Balanced Life: What Is It?" and how everyone will fare differently:

"Imagine a circle cut into eight wedges, where the pieces represent the following key areas in life: career, money, health, friends and family, significant other, personal growth, fun and recreation, and physical environment. Rate your satisfaction in each area of your life from one to ten. Then draw a line in each wedge to symbolize your score, with one being close to the center and ten close to the outer edge.

How smooth is the circle you drew? How bumpy is your life? If you scored everything a one, your ride will be very smooth indeed. Unfortunately, you also won't get very far because your wheel won't cover much ground! What would be a ten for you in each area? No matter where we begin, all the sections of your life are interconnected, just like the wedges on the wheel. It's simply a matter of what you want to focus on first."[73]

In terms of the career portion of the wheel, women who are caretakers cannot disregard the areas of friends and family. They must create a future where those needs are safe, feasible, and met to their satisfaction. Their relationship with any significant other should also prioritize present and future goals.

Ideally, women must make a realistic assessment to determine the ideal number on each individual category now and as the business grows. This tool is one which can best meet a business owner's personal and professional needs, along with the needs of a growing business. You can access more information on the Wheel of Life on my author page on my business MalamaDoe's website.[74]

COLLABORATIVE DECISION-MAKING

As I looked over the Wheel of Life, I noticed where my life, and that of many women with small children, was out of balance. By starting a business as a Flexibility Entrepreneur, I could improve my Wheel of Life now and in the future. As I spent the next year working on this scenario conducting research, I began to roll out my business by leaving the Tier

---

73 Ibid.
74 "Book by Sheila Long," MalamaDoe, accessed April 7, 2021.

of Discovery and entering the Tier of Canvasser. By doing so, I accomplished what Waverly had suggested above:

1. Being bold
2. Remembering how to sell
3. Asking
4. Paying It forward
5. Thinking big

Yet, I had to admit that I was scared. When it comes to fear, I was not alone and soon found out how comfortable I would become with it. For example, when a potential business owner ranks their key areas on the Wheel of Life, fear manifests through every area, especially money. Accepting fear is hard for women, who as studies show below, make decisions differently than men.

Demonstrated research tells us women have more sensitive, considerate, and humble personalities than men. For example, when leaving the initial Tier of **Discovery** and entering the Tier of **Canvasser**, women seek more guidance than men, going online to gain knowledge, fully analyzing their ideas, then facing their fears when courageously voicing, committing, and launching their idea to their inner circle.[75] If they need support to share in caretaking responsibilities, they use social sensitivity to take extra steps and "risk-alert" precautions to focus on reliable winning scenarios. They can then gain a successful outcome involving teamwork and collaboration. The women founders can then

---

75 Tomás Chamorro-Premuzic, "Why Do So Many Incompetent Men Become Leaders?," *Harvard Business Review,* August 22, 2013, accessed March 20, 2021.

find balance, normally as a necessity or flexibility entrepreneur, because they are in a supportive work culture.[76] [77]

While in the Tier of **Canvasser,** founders spend a lot of time working on an intangible business with no revenue or established brand, while keeping those in their inner circle accountable to respecting their work-life boundaries and wishes. It is a very lonely time and requires commitment on behalf of the founders and their inner circle. After attending Booth Women Connect, I spent the next year in the Tier of Canvasser. It took courage, determination, and hard work to take my business and personal life to the next level.

THE CURRENT REALITY OF WOMEN AND CARETAKING

One day, I was working out of my favorite coffee shop, North Shore Boulangerie, a cozy French bakery which has wonderful walk-in traffic for locals with a friendly feel, a great smell of freshly cooked bread, and a wonderful ambiance. A few tables over, an acquaintance from my mom's group named Jessie was working nearby. We began discussing if women who had babies could start businesses.

Jessie looked me straight in the eye and said, "Starting a business from home with small children and no childcare is not reasonable. Women need to have a sitter and, or, a

76 Anita Woolley and Thomas W. Malone, "Defend Your Research: What Makes a Team Smarter? More Women," *Harvard Business Review*, June 2011, accessed February 13, 2021.

77 Kathy Caprino, "How Decision-Making Is Different between Men and Women and Why It Matters in Business," *Forbes*, May 12, 2016, accessed February 13, 2021.

partner who shoulders his part of the load, in addition to ample funds." We agreed that most women do not have the funds to have childcare and start a business without having an additional job.

I remembered what Waverly said about women needing to dominate their industries and continue to work, instead of being a caretaker. Yet, I live in a world where many women are caretakers, disconnected from their network, and find it hard to reconnect. When temporarily deciding to be a caretaker instead of pursuing a full-time career, women may feel alone and afraid when they hear they will take a hit in wage, career advancement, and wealth.[78] These women are not alone. Sixty-five percent of caretakers are women, and they shoulder an immense responsibility to keep those in their charge safe.[79]

A family may not want to outsource caregiving; even if they did, in many cases, it may not make sense. When families evaluate their current and future path on the Wheel of Life, they must meet the needs of many factors, not just financial. Regardless, hiring a caretaker is expensive. Some women have support with caregiving, and some do not. For example, women "handle the most difficult caregiving tasks (i.e., bathing, toileting, and dressing)," with a possibility of spending as much as 50 percent more time providing

---

78 Michael Madowitz, Alex Rowell, and Katie Hamm, *Calculating the Hidden Cost of Interrupting a Career for Child Care* (Washington DC: Center for American Progress, 2016), 1-22.

79 NAC and AARP Public Policy Institute, *2015 Report Caregiving in the U.S., National Alliance for Caregiving and AARP Public Policy Institute* (Washington D.C.: NAC and AARP Public Policy Institute, 2015), 14.

care than men.[80] [81] Some particular caretakers who are especially vulnerable are:

- transplants moving to new locations
- immigrants unfamiliar with local customs
- single parents or only children with no local support
- experience verbal, emotional, physical, and psychological abuse
- professionals disconnected locally
- casualties of betrayal and territorialism
- charged with excessive responsibility which includes:
  - multiple small children in their care
  - special needs and disabled individuals in their care[82]
  - no help given from a partner, neighbor, or family

A caretaker without adequate support walks down a tough road. There are few standards for what constitutes adequate support, and many caretakers are impacted by the above situations. I understand this because I was also one of these women as a transplant and having had three children under the age of five years old. I know full well years of excessive caregiving can dampen the spirit of someone, causing them to feel isolated, incomplete, and inadequate. Yet, as these responsibilities lighten over time, a caregiver can flourish by starting a business.

---

80 NAC and AARP Public Policy Institute, *2015 Report Caregiving in the U.S.*, *National Alliance for Caregiving and AARP Public Policy Institute* (Washington D.C.: NAC and AARP Public Policy Institute, 2015), 8.

81 "Aging in America," Education, Institute on Aging, accessed March 28, 2021.

82 Diana Boesch and Katie Hamm, *Valuing Women's Caregiving During and After the Coronavirus Crisis* (Washington DC: Center for American Progress, 2020), 1-8.

A business owner can be a full-time caregiver with no staff in the first few tiers of **Discovery, Canvasser,** and **Growth** if they are running a proactive business where they control the rate of growth of the company. They will learn incredible multitasking skills. Yet, they must have financial and emotional support to have someone focus adequate time and energy when planning and implementing the business strategy.[83] [84]

When the business becomes reactive, its needs dictate the life of the business owner because the pace of business increases and can no longer be controlled. Sales orders have grown and shifted from 100 percent proactive to 40 percent reactive, with purchasing customers requiring support. Founders are then in the tier of **Prospering.**[85] The founder needs a plan which may include taking on debt to hire staff to run their business. If they launched the business to be a Flexibility Entrepreneur, they need to reassess their goals.

Business owners without staff or caretaking support find the financial strain of running a business taxing at the point. There is no break because of the fast pace of growth. Having a day job, where they could go home at the end of a workday, sounds appealing. However, if they implement a solid plan for support staff, they will grow to a manageable pace and arrive

83   Dayna Winter, "9 Businesses Run by Badass Multitasking Super-
      moms," *Shopify* (blog), May 12, 2017, accessed March 21, 2021.
84   Margo Aaron, "These Women Prove That Having Kids Makes You a
      Better Business Owner, Not a Worse One," *Mother Hustle* (blog), April
      10, 2018, accessed March 21, 2021.
85   Hannah Seligson, "Nurturing a Baby and a Start-up Business," *New York
      Times*, June 9, 2012, accessed March 21, 2021.

in the Tier of Fulfillment where the workload is predictable and manageable.[86]

CARRIE ON THE IMPORTANCE OF A SUPPORTIVE WORK CULTURE

Women choose their workplace based on its accommodation of their life stage in a way men don't. Carrie began her career as a co-op student in college in a STEM position in corporate America when she was childless. She continued her career with them for the next fourteen years.

After the birth of her first child, Carrie realized she had outgrown the company because of the unsupportive workplace for young mothers. After a little over six months of strife with a demanding full-time role and a newborn, she learned reducing her hours would likely impact her performance appraisal, and she courageously left the only workplace she knew. Her company was no longer a good fit and she needed time to rejuvenate and reevaluate her life.

Carrie had a second child, became a stay-at-home mom for two years, cultivated great friendships, and eventually accepted a less demanding part-time role. When her children were older, she found a better paying position that she could use to both support herself and be a mom of school-aged children. She found that the role does not define her; instead it gives her autonomy to express her passions. Carrie is happy now, not waiting for happiness in the future.

---

86   Ibid.

This workplace transition is common and one we can all understand for women as they begin the monumental job of raising young children. Women need to evaluate where they are at on the Wheel of Life. They also need a stable, financially sound, fulfilling career. If they do not have it, they should not be afraid to quit their job to find a better fit. The next story depicts that of a woman whose career flourished after the birth of her children because of the support she had at home.

SAVITA'S AMAZING SUPPORT SYSTEM

Five years ago, I was moderating a seminar called "Managing a Virtual Project" when I first heard of Savita Love. Savita ran all of her projects virtually out of her home in Rochester, New York. After our first phone conversation, I realized her experience would be invaluable to the class. Years later, she told me the full story of what was happening in her life around that time.

"I had my two kids back-to-back. I had postpartum depression with both of them, so I actually struggled." She paused. "I struggled being a mom. But I was really, really good at what I did at work." Her husband noted her plight and stepped in, taking time off of work to help with their young children to support his wife through a troubling time. He knew she would benefit professionally from him being the primary parent. They made it through, and when the time was right, he resumed his career.

Savita now works in a 100 percent virtual role. She enjoys working and evolving through a constantly changing environment. Having a C-Level title is not important to her right now. "What's important is that I have time for me to focus on my career, on my children, and to find a hobby. As a working mom, it's a hard thing trying to figure out how to balance."

SUPPORTING CARETAKERS

Sheryl Sandberg is a very affluent leader for whom funds for childcare is not an issue. She had more than ample financial, emotional, household, and professional support. She was the Facebook COO when she did a TED Talk in 2010 entitled, "Why We Have Too Few Women Leaders," and the overwhelming response lead her to write a book detailing women's struggles.[87] In her book, she acknowledges the challenges of having a career and being a mother.[88] By writing this book, she reminds us of the importance of the feminist revolution.[89] After her book's success, she created Lean In Circles, "a safe space to share your struggles, give and get advice, and celebrate each other's win" to help women find support.[90]

Sheryl also recommends women ask for help in the home and not micromanage it. As with Waverly's comments, I agree this works to a point for women who have support and are not in a vulnerable situation. For the latter, we need to accept and understand the limitations they face.

---

87 Sheryl Sandberg, "Why We Have Too Few Women Leaders," filmed December 2010 in Washington, D.C., TED video, 14:42.

88 Sheryl Sandberg, *Lean In: Women, Work and the Will to Lead* (New York: Knopf, 2013).

89 Susan Adams, "10 Things Sheryl Sandberg Gets Exactly Right in 'Lean In'," *Forbes*, March 4, 2013, accessed February 14, 2021.

90 "Lean In Circles," Lean In, accessed March 31, 2021.

Many caregivers start businesses on the side because they have flexibility, but without adequate understanding, resources, and support from the community, they will have a tougher path. This is where the roles of the necessity and flexibility entrepreneur come in and why their needs are different from that of the opportunity entrepreneur. Caretakers spend "an average of 24.4 hours per week providing care (and) nearly one in four caregivers spend forty-one hours or more per week providing care."[91]

Women need support. Sometimes, a boss can be that person. Here is an incredible story of how the need for support worked out famously for these three people.

MICHELLE OBAMA MEETS MENTOR VALERIE JARRETT

Michelle Obama walked into the City of Chicago's mayor's office for a job interview during a trying time in her life. Over the past year, she had lost her father to a debilitating illness and a close friend. Her emotional support needs were high even though she was in a solid, intimate, supportive relationship. She was looking to leave her successful career in the field of law, which would put her financial and professional support into question. Michelle needed a supportive work culture.

During the interview, she met Valerie Jarrett and was offered the job, yet days later when asked to accept the offer, Michelle demurred, telling her she had concerns after talking it over

---

91 NAC and AARP Public Policy Institute, *2015 Report Caregiving in the U.S., National Alliance for Caregiving and AARP Public Policy Institute* (Washington D.C.: NAC and AARP Public Policy Institute, 2015), 7.

with her soon-to-be husband Barack. Valerie was surprised to hear her potential employee asking for support from her partner but acquiesced to a dinner invitation from Michelle and Barack.[92] [93]

At the dinner, Valerie listened to how Michelle wanted to ensure she did not lose sight of her values if she took the job. Valerie told her, "I will never ask you to do anything you're uncomfortable doing and will stand in the way of anybody who does." Michelle then, knowing she had support, took the job.

In her new role, Michelle learned a lot from Valerie, who had a five-year-old child at the time, about balancing and prioritizing parenting and work. She served as an incredible role model for Michelle. In addition, this working relationship demonstrated the value of support. It also laid the groundwork for Valerie's future as she became Michelle's husband Barack Obama's longest serving senior advisor during his presidency.[94] [95] Our next Awesome Woman had to assess her values and priorities when they did not align, which led to her starting her own business.

92 Valerie Jarrett, "Valerie Jarrett on 26-Year-Old Michelle Obama's Unforgettable Job Interview," *Literary Hub*, accessed February 14, 2021.

93 Michelle Obama, Valerie Jarrett, Dan Fierman, Anna Holmes, and Mukta Mohan, "Working Women: Valerie Jarrett and the Importance of Mentorship," September 30, 2020, in *The Michelle Obama Podcast*, produced by Higher Ground Audio, podcast, MP3 audio, 44:20.

94 Valerie Jarrett, "Valerie Jarrett on 26-Year-Old Michelle Obama's Unforgettable Job Interview," *Literary Hub*, accessed February 14, 2021.

95 Michelle Obama, Valerie Jarrett, Dan Fierman, Anna Holmes, and Mukta Mohan, "Working Women: Valerie Jarrett and the Importance of Mentorship," September 30, 2020, in *The Michelle Obama Podcast*, produced by Higher Ground Audio, podcast, MP3 audio, 44:20.

CINDY MACHLES OWNS HER FUTURE

Seven years ago, Cindy opened up Glue Advertising and Public Relations.[96] She specializes in communicating in very regulated markets and has over twenty years' experience. She has built her business by cultivating client relationships and admits a job switch helped as well. Prior to founding Glue, Cindy "had a very senior job in a big conglomerate organization" and was out of the country on business when her mother had an accident, leaving her sister and father to work out the next steps for her mom.

Cindy explained, "My mother fell and broke her hip. Because she had advanced Alzheimer's, deciding on her future was very difficult. She needed to be placed in a location that may, or may not, have been not satisfactory."

Cindy arrived home for a few days to help, yet she was constantly getting calls from the office. Although she understood how her work "needs me to be in touch," she resented the intrusion in her life. She decided she needed a job switch, with her being able to take a few days off.

She started her company shortly thereafter. She remembers, "If I'm going to work this hard, I'm gonna put myself in a situation where it is my own company, where I'm investing that time and effort in something I'm building for myself."

When she resigned, her boss told her, "I think you're just stressed out."

---

96 "About," Glue Advertising, accessed February 18, 2021.

She replied, "Not really. I handle stress well, it's just time for me now to do this on my own."

As Cindy told me this story, I knew she was not immune to compromised feelings about financial risk. Upon hearing her story, I asked her, "Did you regret it? Even with the sleepless nights?"

"No. In fact, I wished I had done it sooner, but then I wouldn't have as strong a network as I have today. So, it's always hard to know when's the right time to do it. But I am so grateful that I've done it because I have enjoyed these past seven years. I enjoyed the corporate world too. At the point in time that I left, I wasn't enjoying it in the same way."

NEW ZEALAND'S PRIME MINISTER AND MOTHER

Jacinda Ardern is New Zealand's prime minister and became a mother by delivering a baby while running the country. She discusses how she is not abnormal and how she experiences guilt and is torn about parenthood and other typical concerns women face.[97] Yet, because of her leadership role, she can bring her baby to the United Nations General Assembly meeting because she is a nursing mother.[98] Also, in New Zealand, as several other lawmakers had children under the age of one year old, the parliamentary ban on allowing youngsters in the swimming pool was lifted and now there

---

97 Victoria Derbyshire, "New Zealand PM Jacinda Ardern: 'I'm a Mother, Not a Superwoman,'" *BBC News,* video, 1:42.

98 Eleanore Alinge Roy, "Jacinda Ardern Makes History with Baby Neve at Un General Assembly," *The Guardian*, September 24, 2018, accessed February 14, 2021.

is a "parent-child swimming time."[99] By having the support in place for leaders, there is a benefit for all.

Jacinda's partner chose to be a stay-at-home father, and she is fortunate the situation works out best for her family. The below research on navigating a successful career enlightens us about how hard it is when support is lacking.

SPILLOVER AND SUPPORT AT HOME

As we can see from the stories above, caretakers without adequate support must discover life balance somehow. If they do not achieve a professional balance with a supportive work culture, they leave and become a flexibility or necessity entrepreneur.

Two researchers, Evans and Bartolome, conducted a study of two thousand men and reviewed feedback from both them and their spouses. They rolled out the results in a paper entitled "Must Success Cost So Much."

Employees fear financial security because we have to put food on the table for our family, who will suffer the consequences if this cannot be done. Caregivers face their child when there are limited supplies. For this reason, employees are fearful about financial loss and the repercussions about a change in family status.

---

99 Charlotte Graham-McLay, "Jacinda Ardern Embraces Dual Role: New Zealand Prime Minister and Mom," *New York Times*, August 2, 2018, accessed April 9, 2021.

If an employee comes home from work with negative spill-over, their personal life suffers. To combat this, organizations need to ensure their employees achieve balance in their private and professional lives. Organizations must provide supportive work cultures that understand the resources and support their employees' lack.

The personal life of the couple falls on the woman. In a heterosexual relationship, no matter how liberal the couple or how "advanced the culture is, the woman who pursues a career is still expected to be responsible for the quality of the couple's private life." If the woman experiences negative spillover at work, these feelings "spillover into family and leisure time." If the woman is not only in a personal relationship but also a caregiver, the cost of an unsupportive work culture may be too great. With negative spillover, in the worst-case scenario, their "minds are numbed by tension, these people cannot use even their available time in a fulfilling way."[100]

To avoid the above from happening, people may need to change jobs as they shift through their life phases. We do not know what we will, and will not, like in the future. Bartolome and Evans explain, "Much of our behavior is rooted in unconscious motives, and it is difficult to know that part of ourselves. Also, as we age, we are continually changing and gaining new experiences. So, even under the best of circumstances, to assess whether one will fit with a new job is difficult."

---

100 Fernando Bartolomé and Paul A. Lee Evans, "Why Must Success Cost So Much," *Harvard Business Review*, March 1980.

To make it easier, we may start our own business to have the certainty of having a supportive work culture. We seek to find a perfect fit where we have a job we can do well, one we love doing, and one which aligns with our morals where our "work and... moral values coincide."[101]

We need to be happy. We need to survive; thus, we must carve a workable path. We strive to keep our marriages intact. As a perfect fit is not readily found in the workplace, we find a plethora of flexibility and necessity entrepreneurs.

WHEN SUPPORT DISAPPEARS: GROWING AND SHRINKING YOUR BUSINESS

A truly vulnerable caretaker is one who cares for a child with special needs or learning disabilities. They may find their independence stifled. A mother may become a homemaker, if she has not already, to care for the child. Support is defined differently with children with learning disabilities in our lives.

My friend Maggie is a stellar example for all women to follow who understands well the impact of having children with special needs. Maggie is the mother of two wonderful middle-school-aged boys. She is also the stepmother to adult children, one who lives with her. When her children were in school full time, she was able to start a business for the underserved plus-size women's market to have well-fitting clothing. She created a business plan, then a logo and a tagline, and officially announced the opening of her online

---

101 Ibid.

clothing boutique for women size twelve to twenty-two.[102] Over time, she learned to sell on Amazon, rented a storage space, and posted daily videos online dressed in her products and showcasing them to the masses. Her business entered the Tier of Growth and she became a true inspiration to all.

Then, COVID-19 hit in 2020 and her children were sent home from school. Maggie no longer had the professional balance and supportive work culture she once had. Nine months into the pandemic, she lacked the adequate support for her to continue as she had. Her business had taken a huge hit because of the pandemic, and her children were not thriving with remote learning. Realizing the lack of educational support left her with little professional balance, Maggie needed a new plan. With an unpredictable school year ahead of her, she downsized her business to care for her children with a home-schooling routine. Maggie placed her professional dreams on hold because of her new workplace and personal reality.

NEW CONSTITUTIONAL AMENDMENT

Each of these stories depicts how the impact of having support in the workplace and at home matters. Women need to advocate for themselves with a self-assessment tool such as the Wheel of Life and must not be afraid to quit their job and find a better fit elsewhere if required for balance. Caretakers without adequate support leave their careers and discover balance elsewhere, many times as necessity and flexibility entrepreneurs. These women face a new reality, which can be exciting and terrifying at the same time.

---

102 "About Us," Three Wrens, accessed March 28, 2021.

As women take courageous steps to own their destiny, we must help them create a future where they will be fulfilled and make an impact in an area that matters to them. Women leave their careers and start over because they do not have the needed balance, support, and fulfillment in their careers and start over professionally. We must change this by being supportive of the new constitutional amendment and fighting for equal rights. Let's work for the passage of the Equal Rights Amendment to defeat explicit bias, gross injustice, and unacceptable and blatant sexism.

With more support for caretakers by passing the Equal Right Amendment Phyllis so avidly worked against, caretakers can live a more balanced livelihood without feeling pressured into becoming entrepreneurs because it is their only viable alternative. We give women a fair chance when we join their voices with the Times' Up movement and elect women to the US Congress.[103] The ERA Coalition formed with the goal of reintroducing this legislation; let's join the movement to make a change for the betterment of our society.[104] With the ratification of the passage of the ERA Amendments in Nevada in 2017, Illinois in 2018, and Virginia in 2020, the possibility of creating an amendment to the US Constitution prohibiting gender-based discrimination is attainable.

Imagine living in the United States where the wishes of 94 percent of those surveyed who support the passage of this amendment are heard.

---

103 Alex Cohen and Wilfred U. Codrington III, "The Equal Rights Amendment Explained," Our Work, Research & Reports, *Brennan Center for Justice,* January 23, 2020, accessed February 9, 2021.

104 "About the Coalition," ERA Coalition, accessed March 28, 2021.

Imagine having the wage gap eliminated, where women earning seventy-nine cents for each dollar a white man earns and Latinas earning fifty-three cents for each dollar are a distant memory.

Imaging having sexual assaults decrease from every ninety-two seconds, effectively empowering the survivors with rights.[105]

Imagine if we could enact equal rights and rectify the problems which hinder women's professional development, from

- post-partum depression
- care for our loved ones, young and old
- equal pay laws and rights for employees
- professional work cultures that support us

Give us all a break, let's pass the ERA.

---

105 "Home," ERA Coalition, accessed March 28, 2021.

CHAPTER FIVE

Institutional Betrayal Ignites the Courage Within

___

DIRECTING THE NEWS DIFFERENTLY & INSTITUTIONAL BETRAYAL

"That producer is too nasty. We cannot have her directing live television broadcasts. She is so bossy; I would even call it shrill." Annie, who was a director of a national news program, sat back in horror as she heard the feedback given about a female colleague who was excellent at her job.

The others listening agreed, "Yes, her tone is quite sharp. We just cannot give her more responsibility. She is way too authoritative."

Annie had heard similar feedback before, and her heart went out to her colleague. She understood. Annie felt she had never been treated as well as her male counterparts. She was largely passed over for promotion, despite her reputation as an excellent director. What Annie was feeling was a sense of betrayal, something she knew well.

"Betrayal is an emotional reaction similar to a live wire that's been cut. Betrayal impacts our ability to trust, collaborate, reach out, be vulnerable or have a strong sense of self or confidence. Betrayal takes away something that was a part of us."

PATTY TRINKO, NWYZE[106]

Betrayal is tough. Yet, betrayal manifests itself at all ages. When I asked my three school-age children for examples of betrayal, they gave me nonstop ideas, including when someone:

- chooses to not hang out with you
- spreads lies about you
- reveals your secrets
- gossips about you
- ignores you
- dumps you

---

106 Patty Trinko, e-mail message to author, August 24, 2020.

I had no idea they knew betrayal so well, yet I should not have been surprised as it is a part of life. In some ways, we become numb to it as we experience minor social infractions. Betrayal can happen between roommates, family members, friends, colleagues, classmates, or strangers. It can be intentional, habitual, or accidental and can be exacerbated with alcohol or when new parties come into our lives. Whether or not we like it, betrayal happens. Survivors mourn their lost relationships and suffer with an impacted inability to connect.

"The process to repair, after betrayal, is about reaching back IN to find that piece of ourselves that was lost. If we were all raised to talk about our emotions actively and work through emotional dysregulation regularly, then, when betrayal hits, we would know what to do with it."

PATTY TRINKO, NWYZE[107]

A woman who experienced betrayal after spending many years with her employer began the Women's Leadership Podcast, which has a season on it called the Heroine's Journey. I listened to an episode about betrayal where she, the host,

107 Ibid.

tells the story of how she was laid off after being passed over for a promotion. She explained:

"Betrayal is not something we want to experience, because it brings with it all the fear, anger, sadness, and shame. Betrayal can feel like failure, if we view it only through the eyes of traditional models of leadership. But betrayal is also a pivotal moment of choice, where the breaking point is suddenly obvious, and our decision becomes clear. Betrayal is imperative because it shatters our illusions and takes us down the Heroine's Journey path to transformation."

ELIZABETH MCLAUGHLIN[108]

Annie had worked her way up the career ladder directing television news at ABC News for thirty-three years.[109] She was a standout and won two Emmy Awards for her work, which included directing national news programs such as *World*

---

108 Elizabeth McLaughlin, "The Heroine's Journey: Betrayal," Gaia Leadership Project, accessed February 8, 2021.

109 "Home," ABC News, accessed February 6, 2021.

News Tonight, 20/20, and *Nightline.* Annie remembers that the culture was intense due largely to the male dominance of the industry and demand for television ratings. Eventually, she knew she needed to leave network television. It is a move she has never regretted.

About a year after leaving her career, Annie began working as a freelance director for WNET Thirteen, which is the flagship station of PBS.[110] [111] In 2017, she was offered a staff position, instead of freelance, even though she was over sixty! She now directs a variety of shows there, including the national shows of *Amanpour & Company* and *Firing Line with Margaret Hoover.* Annie also has branched out and is involved with many arts events in the fields of music and dance. She describes the difference as incredible. She tells me, "There is no abuse, no discrimination. People are praised for their good work and appreciated." She has loved being a mentor to others as well. Annie now comes home every night feeling like she is part of a great team and embraces an incredible sense of belonging. She is thrilled and feels rewarded with the output of her work.[112] [113]

Annie exited her business working as a freelancer because a client hired her for a full-time role. This happens a lot with business owners when they arrive at the Tier of Prospering. They know how to do their job well and have one or two

---

110 "Home," WNET Thirteen, accessed February 6, 2021.

111 "Home," PBS, accessed February 6, 2021.

112 "Live from the Control Room: News Directors in Conversation," Events, Directors Guild of America, September 27, 2018.

113 "Live from the Control Room: Ann Benjamin," produced by the Directors Guild of America, *Directors Guild of America,* September 27, 2018, video, 1:02.

main clients who take up most of their time. They decide to become their client's employee, leaving the pressures of business ownership, which include hiring more staff and partnering with other groups to grow.

In Annie's case, because of her expertise in the industry, she was in the Tier of Fulfillment. For Annie, opening a business as a contractor allowed her to stay in the workplace and not search for a full-time position. She could proactively work on getting hired, but on her own terms as a business owner.

Annie benefited from all of those years of work on network television. Yet, she can never recover from her time spent in an unsupportive work environment. What happened in network television for Annie happens in many outdated companies. The inherent problems in an industry, be it sexism or racism alongside the assistance of the Boys' Club, must be addressed. If they are not, the organization may be responsible for perpetuating institutional betrayal.

"**Institutional Betrayal** occurs when the institution you trust or depend upon mistreats you. It can be overt, but it can also be less obvious, for instance, a failure to protect you when protection is a reasonable expectation. Our research shows that

> institutional betrayal is also related to measurable harm—again both mental and physical."

JENNIFER J. FREYD, PHD, FOUNDER AND PRESIDENT OF THE CENTER FOR INSTITUTIONAL COURAGE, INC.[114]

In a blog written discussing the courage needed to address institutional betrayal, the nationally known betrayal researcher Jennifer Freyd expressed concern, saying, "It's urgent that we address distrust by helping organizations become more trustworthy. I believe that if we get our institutions behaving in a trustworthy way, that trust will come back."[115]

AWAKE FROM BETRAYAL TRAUMA

The United States Catholic Church's failure to take collective action after over "11,000 accusations of childhood sexual abuse" since the 1970s caused an immense breach of trust. Where I live, in the Archdiocese of Milwaukee, there was an estimated 21-million-dollar settlement to compensate 330 sexual assault survivors."[116] Regardless, the aftermath of the inaction was felt deeply.

---

114 Jennifer J. Freyd, PhD, "Research," accessed February 6, 2021.

115 Erin O'Donnell, "5 Ways the Catholic Church Can Build More 'Institutional Courage,'" *Awake Milwaukee* (blog), September 30, 2020, accessed February 7, 2021.

116 Erica Jones, "Clergy Sexual Abuse Cases Still Rising," *Urban Milwaukee*, November 17, 2019, accessed February 7, 2021.

Sara Larson made a life-altering choice after meeting with some parties saddened, angered, and concerned about the church's role in the sexual abuse. She left her career working in parish ministry to devote herself full time to stopping the institutional betrayal and working for accountability of sexual abuse in the Catholic Church within the Archdiocese of Milwaukee. Over time, the group Awake Milwaukee was formed with the tagline, "Now is the time to awake from sleep."[117]

The group crafted an Open Letter to Survivors offering an apology for any abuse endured in the Church. The letter acknowledges the betrayal those abused experienced when they were not fully heard because church members "didn't listen, doubted you, or lacked the courage to act." To date, over 325 supporters have found the letter on the Awake Milwaukee website and signed it, in an act of future solidarity with the survivors.[118]

Over the past two years since this initial meeting, Sara has become the executive director of Awake Milwaukee, which is now a 501(c). Awake Milwaukee aims to use the goals of listening, learning, and leading the group to realize the full reality of the abuse and work for change. Awake Milwaukee falls in the Tier of Growth.

Awake Milwaukee now has a board of directors and nine members on the leadership team, and Sara acknowledges the abused survivors as being "these brave men and women (who) are the reason behind everything I do with Awake."

---

117 "Home," Awake Milwaukee, accessed April 5, 2021.
118 "Sign Awake's Open Letter to Survivors," The Letter, Awake Milwaukee, accessed April 5, 2021.

Sara is happy she listened to the divine call she received to lead and looks forward to working for change.[119]

What happened to many survivors in the church abuse scandal has also happened to others in different areas. If survivors cannot trust others and betrayal happens repeatedly, we experience betrayal trauma, which, according to expert Jennifer Freyd, impacts our ability to trust our instincts and participate in daily life.[120]

"A **betrayal trauma** occurs when someone you trust and/or someone who has power over you mistreats you. For instance, it's a betrayal trauma when your boss sexually harasses you. Our research shows that betrayal traumas are toxic. They are associated with measurable harm, both physical and mental."

JENNIFER J. FREYD, PHD, FOUNDER AND PRESIDENT OF THE CENTER FOR INSTITUTIONAL COURAGE, INC.[121]

---

119 "Leadership," Who We Are, Awake Milwaukee, accessed March 2, 2021.
120 Jennifer Freyd and Pamela Birrell, *Blind to Betrayal: Why We Fool Ourselves We Aren't Being Fooled* (Hoboken: Wiley, 2013), 261.
121 Jennifer J. Freyd, PhD, "Research," accessed February 6, 2021.

Sometimes, the betrayal is coupled with someone who wants to maintain power over their territory. Our next Awesome Woman, Jen Schwartz, knows this experience all too well.

JEN SCHWARTZ & BETRAYAL BLINDNESS

Jen is a military wife. She had traveled with her husband and relocated to many places. Eventually, her happy family returned to her hometown when their child was school age. Jen applied and was hired at a male-dominated engineering firm in an administrative role. She was happy to be employed and not looking to be promoted.

Her position was a frontline-facing role dealing with clients, and she always made an effort to look professional. On a regular basis, women, not men, made comments about her personal appearance with references about her figure, hair, and clothing, including "backhanded compliments" about the size of her chest or how her pants fit. She found them odd and felt harassed.

Instead of facing problems working with the men in a male-dominated company, Jen was surprised to encounter difficulties working with the women. She felt a true "eat or be eaten" mentality. Despite her constant verbal support and encouragement of female executives and engineers, Jen never felt treated with the same respect. She noticed women executives were competitive, jealous, and fearful among themselves about losing their standing or powers with the men. They would lash out at her. She remembered, "It was awful to be made to feel 'less than' by another woman in an already male-dominated environment." What Jen was experiencing has a name, defined again by Jennifer Freyd: betrayal blindness.

"**Betrayal blindness**, a key concept of betrayal trauma theory, is the unaware-ness, not-knowing, and forgetting exhib-ited by people towards betrayal. Victims, perpetrators, and witnesses may display betrayal blindness in order to preserve relationships, institutions, and social systems upon which they depend."

JENNIFER J. FREYD, PHD, FOUNDER AND PRESIDENT OF THE CENTER FOR INSTITUTIONAL COURAGE, INC.[122]

Yet, some people would rather not admit to, or acknowledge, the betrayal. They are "groomed" to keep quiet about any injustice they see, which leads to betrayal blindness. My colleague Patty believes women cannot ignore the role of sexism and we must walk a tightrope in business.

"The patriarchal system supports men's ideas so much more than women. It also supports sexual innuendo as a 'natural way of engaging' at work. Women are also

---

122 Ibid.

labeled as emotional, so they often don't get support for what they need when the betrayal happens. I have experienced this myself and found both male and female managers were guilty of these examples."

PATTY TRINKO, NWYZE[123]

Betrayal is a part of our everyday existence, and learning to survive within its confines can be an everyday reality for many. Thankfully, Jen was able to leave her position where she did not feel comfortable and change her daily work atmosphere for the better. She left this company after founding a start-up, Therapeutic Massage by Jen.[124] This move was happenstance as she began taking massage classes as a hobby yet found an incredible mentor who encouraged her to look at it as a career choice. After a key introduction by her mentor, she became a business owner when her service was needed within the walls of a complementary business that needed her skill set. Jen's business is in the Tier of Growth. Nowadays, she remembers the strange nature of her former workplace where her female colleagues made such odd, upsetting, and hurtful comments and is glad they are no longer part of her daily reality.

---

123 Ibid.

124 Therapeutic Massage by Jen, LLC, "Now Booking Appointments," Facebook, July 19, 2020, accessed February 7, 2021.

According to Forbes, women fear other women a lot. Just the mere thought of potential sabotage from other women who will inevitably undermine their abilities causes another woman's reluctance to put forth any effort to succeed.[125] The need to sabotage another woman may have roots in an unstable marriage, job, or plain insecurity. When women become territorial in this way, one woman's fear stops another woman from moving forward. A great way to intervene is to befriend the offending women, to talk to a supportive women's group, or to approach a leader in the organization.

RETAIL FORTUNE 500 COMPANIES HAVE WOMEN CEOS

If we want to see women progress, the number of industries where women are misfits and thus ill-suited for a thriving long-term career is a major obstacle. Until this feeling of being a "misfit" is rectified, the few women who enter these fields will continue to exit these industries as they are not set up for them. Women's voices will not be a factor when decisions are made because they will not be at the table, in the boardrooms and CEO positions at Fortune 500 companies.

One place where women do fit is in the retail industry, as they can find their bearings, easily navigate it, and feel they belong. In 2021, of the Fortune 500 companies, there will soon be forty-one women CEOs in retail, or 8 percent of all CEOs.[126]

125 Lidija Globokar, "What Are Women Most Afraid Of?," *Forbes,* March 8, 2019, accessed March 28, 2021.

126 Lauren Thomas, "The Retail Industry Is Leading the Way as Women Take over CEO Roles," *CNBC,* December 28, 2020, accessed January 28, 2020.

WHICH TEXTURE IS YOUR CEILING?

Retail is only one of the twenty-one sectors represented in the Fortune 500 listing. For the remaining twenty sectors, women may not feel they fit into the cultures. If women attempt to work in places where they do not belong, they may not have the energy or desire to continue.[127]

This lack of representation of women in 95 percent of the sectors in the Fortune 500 reminds me of the 1979 term *the glass ceiling* coined to refer to ceilings made of glass. The texture continued to evolve for how misfits could not become leaders in companies, with variations of ceilings being a "bamboo ceiling" (for Asian-Americans), a "celluloid ceiling" (for women in Hollywood) and a "marble ceiling" (for women in government).[128] Some black, Indigenous, and people of color (BIPOC) communities have called the ceiling cement as well.[129] Nowadays, non-BIPOC communities are feeling the actual texture of the ceiling. As they are realizing it is definitely not glass, they are getting on board with the wave of change blanketing our country, a wave of inclusivity for all women.

OWNING YOUR POWER & ACCEPTING THE BETRAYAL OF TERRITORIALISM THEN & NOW

For us to be inclusive to women, we need to make peace with other women. Anne, the Opportunity Entrepreneur we

---

127 "Fortune 500," Fortune, accessed January 28, 2020.

128 Ben Zimmer, "The Phrase 'Glass Ceiling' Stretches Back Decades," *The Wall Street Journal*, April 3, 2015, accessed January 24, 2021.

129 Jo-Ann Tan, "For Women of Color, the Glass Ceiling is Actually Made of Concrete," *HuffPost* (blog), April 20, 2016.

met in Chapter Three, was one of the early entrants to the new field of financial planning. Anne and I discussed how times have changed. Anne noticed how now, in financial services, female advisors "lift each other up" when meeting annually, form friendships, and help each other out with work-life balance concerns as well as promote sharing of best business practices. We find that today young professionals can drop their guard easier and provide more of a refuge for each other, the opposite of the early days when women were more strongly competing for business leadership roles.

To ensure I can be a person who also lifts others up, every year I return to my alma mater, the University of Chicago Booth School of Business, to attend their annual Booth Women Connect Conference.[130] I thrive in this setting, where we hear from leaders in academia and business. After being inspired by multiple success stories, I leave prepared to craft a workable career development strategy.

One year, when selecting my seminars, I decided, along with over two hundred other women, to attend a popular MBA professor Tanya Menon, PhD's, talk, "Women in Business: You are a Threat—Own It."[131] Tanya enlightened me by verifying how women experience a lack of support in the workplace as leaders, and how we must address it when it happens to us. Tanya says that business meeting rooms are filled with

130 "Booth Women Connect," The University of Chicago Booth School of Business, accessed March 28, 2021.

131 Tanya Menon, "Women in Business: You're a Threat, Own It!" (Powerpoint Presentation, 5th Annual Booth Women Connect Conference, Booth Women Connect, Chicago, IL, October 23, 2015).

aggressive personalities, some who have earned little respect professionally, or status, and attempt to undermine others, especially women, with power plays.

Tanya reminded us to use strategies such as humor to gain power by building and lining up allies to use the power of the group and social norms to boost our status during future power plays. Humor is especially useful when the aggressive personality uses DARVO, which stands for Deny, Attack, and Reverse Victim and Offender. DARVO is an effective tool used when being held accountable and a challenging one for any experiencing the repercussions of betrayal:

"Perpetrators and their defenders may <u>D</u>eny the behavior, <u>A</u>ttack the victim confronting them, and <u>R</u>everse the roles of <u>V</u>ictim and <u>O</u>ffender. In this way, a perpetrator can adopt the victim role and accuse the true victim of being an offender."

CENTER FOR INSTITUTIONAL COURAGE[132]

---

132 "Knowledge Base and Research Priorities," Research, Center for Institutional Courage, accessed March 28, 2021.

However, when humor is applied, it may be counter-acted. Tanya acknowledged that without a network, everything is more challenging as we cannot gain power and other networks will be respected over ours. Status and power are connected. When we are in the midst of power plays to gain status, we must use our network and the power of the group to build up allies. Yet, our status cannot be changed if we ignore how gender plays a big part in how we can exhibit emotions. We discuss this further in Chapter Nine.

As we can see, women face betrayal and territorialism in a traditional workplace. It is hard to imagine any sane women choosing a situation with rampant requirements set upon us based on our femininity, emotional expressions, marital status, childcare situation, and more. With regard to the Confidence Gap, women find themselves in a no-win situation. We discuss this more in Chapter Ten.

GROWING FROM BETRAYAL

Whether we have been betrayed in the home, the workplace, or the community, we need love, safety, and trust.[133] Whether it be:

- realizing lost time spent in an unfulfilling setting
- healing from the sadness of an unsettling relationship
- accepting our role in institutional betrayal
- surviving the wrath of women blind to their own betrayal
- recovering from a toxic boss after experiencing betrayal trauma

---

133 Jennifer Freyd and Pamela Birrell, *Blind to Betrayal: Why We Fool Ourselves We Aren't Being Fooled* (Hoboken: Wiley, 2013), 334.

To grow from the experience, and to heal, we must share what happened with a trusted individual with active listening skills so we can connect internally and externally. This enables us to become bonded with others. By doing so, we can navigate a new this newfound path, while remembering the path we went down before, and "honor the process and shape (our) future."[134]

By being in an unfamiliar environment, such as starting a business, we have time to grow and heal and face the stigma of what happened to us. It can liberate us from the betrayal. We can stop the painful situation we were in and make plans to move forward, all the while protecting more valuable relationships. We can do this by working together with other female business owners to grow, heal, and move forward on a more fruitful path.

---

134 Freyd and Pamela Birrell, *Blind to Betrayal*, 329.

CHAPTER SIX

Misfits Awaken and Sidepreneurs Embark

———

NADIYAH JOHNSON: DOWN TO MARS

"I cannot concentrate. Please tame your hair for your presentations going forward."

Nadiyah Johnson, a young data analyst interning in a large company, was stunned when after doing an impressive presentation for her manager, she was pulled aside and given feedback by her manager that her hair was a distraction. Nadiyah, a black woman, was speechless. This was her first lesson in the different standards for hair in a business setting for BIPOC and white women. Since she was one of a few black women working there, she understood it to mean that she "could not be her authentic self." Thankfully, this experience did not cause her to leave the field of technology.[135] [136] She continued her work without any hairstyle modifications but took note that she had limited BIPOC representatives around her.

Hair discrimination, which really has to do with inclusion and ensuring we accept everyone, is not acceptable. The creation of The Crown Act, or Creating a Respectful and Open World for Natural Hair Act, and its passage prohibit discrimination in schools and workplaces based on hair texture and hairstyle. Legislation was passed in many states and signed by the US House of Representatives on September 12, 2020, and is under review in the US Senate.[137] To show your support, please go the website with the name The Crown Act.[138]

Few people wait for a company to build a culture that meets their needs. Instead, they leave their full-time jobs and create an opportunity that works. For Nadiyah, her experience as a misfit inspired her to become a sidepreneuer. When she heard the city of Milwaukee was working toward becoming a tech hub, she was thrilled as she works in technology. Simultaneously, Nadiyah also knew the national narrative about how Milwaukee, which is 65 percent BIPOC and 35

---

135 Nadiyah Johnson, "Episode 11 - The Young Shall Lead Them - Host Jordan Davis," November 3, 2019, in *Down to Mars,* produced by Nadiyah Johnson, podcast, MP3 audio, 23:25, accessed April 4, 2021.

136 Nadiyah Johnson, "BIT TechTalk ep. 121 w/ Nadiyah Johnson of Jet Constellations," June 2, 2020, in *Tech Talk Blacks in Technology,* produced by Blacks in Technology, podcast, MP3 audio, 60:32.

137 Kiara McClendon, "The Crown Act Makes Waves across the Country to End Hair Discrimination," *Forbes,* January 13, 2021, accessed March 23, 2021.

138 "Home," The Crown Act, accessed March 23, 2021.

percent white, was the most segregated city for the BIPOC community nationwide. As Nadiyah regularity navigated both environments, she knew black voices could thrive locally, especially in tech, otherwise known as STEM. However, Nadiyah knew the caveat for it working was that the environment could only thrive in a safe space.[139]

Nadiyah took action founding a business doing just that while keeping her day job. Now, at twenty-eight years old, she is a rising star.[140] She runs her start-up, Jet Constellations, a "fast-growing software company providing tech solutions in medical, financial, and socially responsibly industries."[141] After opening it, she was invited by local tech hub leaders to enter rooms where decisions were made. As a data scientist by trade and active in academia, she noted the data of the individuals present. Basically, there were very few women and "no black people in the room."[142] To combat this inequity, she founded a social impact arm of Jet Constellations, naming it the Milky Way Tech Hub, as "an initiative to transform Milwaukee and other cities into diverse tech hubs that represent the landscape of the city."[143]

139 Nadiyah Johnson, "Stars Tell a Story," filmed October 2020 at TEDx-MarquetteU, Milwaukee, WI, video, 15:01.

140 Carole Meekins, "Milwaukee Woman Works to Expand Tech Opportunities in the City," Positively Milwaukee, *TMJ4*, May 3, 2019, accessed January 24, 2021.

141 "Home," Jet Constellations, accessed January 24, 2021.

142 Nadiyah Johnson, "Stars Tell a Story," filmed October 2020 at TEDx-MarquetteU, Milwaukee, WI, video, 15:01.

143 Nadiyah Johnson, "BITTechTalk ep. 121 w/ Nadiyah Johnson of Jet Constellations," June 2, 2020, in *Tech Talk Blacks in Technology*, produced by Blacks in Technology, podcast, MP3 audio, 60:32.

Her Milky Way Tech Hub "launched a fifty-million-dollar fund to invest in tech companies owned by minorities."[144] In September 2020, Nadiyah was part of a Build Back Better roundtable with Kamala Harris.[145] Months later and days after Vice President Kamala Harris was sworn into office, Nadiyah, along with a group of leaders from across the country, was invited to share how she is helping local businesses deal with the pandemic.[146] Nadiyah feels she belongs in a community of her own creation.

DEFINING A CAREER MISFIT

Two researchers, Evans and Bartolome, talk about a career misfit often in their paper, "Must Success Cost So Much." Here is how they define it:

"A perfect fit occurs when you experience three positive feelings at the same time: you feel competent, you enjoy the work, and you feel that your work and your moral

---

144 Brandon Anderegg, "Milky Way Tech Hub to Launch $50 Million Fund to Invest In Tech Companies Owned By Minorities," *BizTimes*, June 24, 2020, accessed April 12, 2021.

145 WisPolitics, "Biden Campaign: Following Kamala Harris' Visit, Milwaukee Black Business Owners Praise Build Back Better Plan," WisPolitics Press Release, September 9, 2020, on the WisPolitics website, accessed April 4, 2021.

146 Bianca Shaw, "Founder of Milky Way Tech Hub Meets Vice President Kamala Harris on Second Day in Office," *Milky Way Tech Hub* (blog), January 24, 2021, accessed April 4, 2021.

values coincide. To express this in another way, a job should fit not only with skills and abilities but also with motives and values. A misfit situation occurs whenever one of these three conditions is absent. In the case of the *total misfit,* none of the conditions is fulfilled: he is not particularly competent at what he does, he enjoys few aspects of his work, and he feels ashamed doing things that go against his values or ideals."

If a job is not one we can do well, one we love doing, and one which aligns with our morals, this job is a misfit. There are three types of misfits: "competence," "employment," and "moral."[147] If employees do not feel they belong at work, otherwise known as a job misfit, they will leave. They may fill out a business model canvas for their exit plan and become a sideprenuer.

Nadiyah may have been experiencing a moral misfit when opening Jet Constellations. Yet even though she brings the traction of additional women entering the world of technology, the reality is that many women exit. In technology, one can find a plethora of women in a job misfit.

---

147 Fernando Bartolomé and Paul A. Lee Evans, "Why Must Success Cost So Much," *Harvard Business Review,* March 1980.

TECHNOLOGY, WOMEN, & COMPUTERS

Women have an intricate past in technology. Yet, many of their stories were not told. Before delving into why, let's explore what exactly is technology. The definition from *Encyclopedia Britannica* states it is "the development over time of systematic techniques for making and doing things."[148] Technology was first used with a focus on the arts in the seventeenth century, yet:

"By the early 20th century, the term (technology) embraced a growing range of means, processes and ideas in addition to tools and machines."

ROBERT ANGUS BUCHANAN[149]

One of technology's machines is the computer, whose idea spun from the mind of a brilliant female mathematician, Ada Lovelace. Ada was born into a wealthy, noble family and was educated by private tutors. As an adult, she wanted to continue to develop her mathematical skills, a career misfit for a woman of her stature. Yet, as she lived a balanced, supported, and fulfilled life, she was fortunate to develop herself professionally. In 1842, Ada placed numbers into what would

---

148 Robert Angus Buchanan, "History of Technology," *Encyclopedia Britannica,* November 18, 2020, accessed March 23, 2021.

149 Ibid.

be the first program for a mechanical computer, envisioning the current computer with "four components of its design - input, storage, processing, and output."[150]

"Ada Lovelace had made the mental leap from hardware to software...A computer that does only one thing isn't a really a computer. It is just a machine."

CLAIRE L. EVANS, AUTHOR OF *BROAD BAND: THE UNTOLD STORY OF THE WOMEN WHO MADE THE INTERNET.*[151]

Ada's ideas led to inventions allowing workers to take in information, analyze it, and solve problems which were managed by primarily women called "human computers." From the telephone operators working in the 1890s, to the typists and punch card operators in the 1940s, and all those in between, these roles required someone with a "keen analytical mind and limitless patience." They kept records, collaborated, and evolved while manipulating information and their subsequent networks for both the inside and outside of machines.[152] As this criterion is where women historically

---

150 Claire L. Evans, *Broad Band: The Untold Story of the Women Who Made the Internet* (New York: Portfolio, 2018), 25-29, Kindle.

151 Evans, *Broad Band: The Untold Story of the Women Who Made the Internet,* 95.

152 Evans, *Broad Band: The Untold Story of the Women Who Made the Internet,* 31-36.

excel, ideally the career fit was one for their competence and employment, yet may or may not have been a moral fit.

MISSED RECOGNITION FOR SMART TRAILBLAZING WOMEN

A century later, in the 1940s, intelligent women with mathematical abilities similar to Ada Lovelace but with dissimilar levels of balance and support were challenged to find intellectually fulfilling careers. They, like Ada, were also viewed as misfits by society and realized there were few employment opportunities to use their mathematical skills.[153] To combat living an unbalanced, unfulfilled professional life, six smart women joined the military and became human computers working on the ENIAC, "the most powerful calculating device built to date." The women were called the Eniac Six, and their accomplishments operating this massive machine by "moving wires and creating programs" became the advent of the modern-day field known as computer software programming.

Professionally, they were incredibly competent and challenged. The most competent of all six was the tough and influential, determined, opinionated, yet charismatic programmer Betty Jean Bartik. Unfortunately, the work of Betty Jean and the Eniac Six received little recognition as the public barely comprehended the hardware, so their intangible software work was inexplicable and unrecognizable to an outsider. Regardless, the Eniac Six knew they belonged and

---

153 Evans, *Broad Band: The Untold Story of the Women Who Made the Internet*, 57.

were fulfilled at their work, yet they did not receive the necessary support or balance.[154] [155]

Another incredibly mathematically talented programmer was Grace Hopper, a PhD in math from Yale. She laid the groundwork in the computing culture to ensure a competitive environment that drove internal competition did not proliferate, but instead a culture where "competitors, programmers, professional organizations, the military and clients" worked collaboratively did. In doing so, she predated mainstream ideas by thirty years by recognizing the value of the teamwork.[156] [157]

"Hopper's belief that programs should be written in a language that was close to English (rather than in machine code or in languages close to machine code, such as assembly languages) was captured in the new business language."

HISTORY OF SCIENTIFIC WOMEN[158]

154 Evans, *Broad Band: The Untold Story of the Women Who Made the Internet*, 66-68.
155 "Home," Eniac Programmers, accessed March 23, 2021.
156 Evans, *Broad Band: The Untold Story of the Women Who Made the Internet*, 37, 93.
157 "Grace Hopper," History of Scientific Women, accessed March 23, 2021.
158 Ibid.

Until recently, history books have ignored the work of these women and many other programmers. In hindsight, the Eniac Six, Betty Jean, Grace, and others were awarded. A researcher, Kathy Kleinman, has been instrumental in correcting the oversights and ensuring their accomplishments are recognized.[159]

"Jean Bartik's contributions to computing are significant, and still largely undocumented. I want Jean Bartik to be a name known to every girl and boy who studies computing. I want her to be a role model for the next generations. She's a real inspiration."

KATHY KLEIMAN, PRODUCER OF ENAIC PROGRAMMERS[160]

The moral misfit in the employment of women in technology became apparent in the 1960s: as computers entered mainstream society and technology advanced, it created the need for more programmers.

159 "Home," Eniac Programmers, accessed March 23, 2021.
160 Kirk L. Kroeker, "Remembering Jean Bartik," *ACM News*, April 19, 2011, accessed March 23, 2021.

FORMALIZING WOMEN'S EXCLUSION IN TECHNOLOGY

Programmers need to have their work, which is categorized as projects, run on time, within budget, and according to specifications: the exact requirements where Grace Hopper, the Eniac Six, Jean Bartik, and women then and now excel. Computer scientists appreciate knowing problems will be communicated and resolved effectively. They value colleagues who provide a clear understanding of users' needs and outcomes with effective social communication skills.[161]

Unfortunately, the field of computer programming was formalized and placed into the realm of the male-dominated field of software engineering. This move ostracized women workers, who were already penalized for the inherent inequities in the professional world of pay, gender, and sexism. Women, who excelled in the programming role in dire need of being filled, no longer belonged.[162]

Further exacerbating their exclusion, an aptitude test was conducted to best define the "clear requirements" needed to succeed as a programmer. The test, done primarily on the male programmers, revealed the ideal programmer traits needed, including someone who "liked solving puzzles" but didn't "like people." These qualifications were in contrast to the main components to running successful projects of soft skills and collaboration, requirements needed for successful and efficient computer programming.

---

161 Evans, *Broad Band: The Untold Story of the Women Who Made the Internet*, 99.

162 Ibid.

Unfortunately, industry recruiters then screened and hired programmers who were loners that solved problems. The recruiters found more men met the antisocial requirement because society celebrates more men for being the "lone wolf," as compared to woman, who are shunned for being "socially inept." The recruiters subsequently hired primarily men in the 1960s and 1970s.

Consequently, in the 1980s, the male managers who rose in the ranks hired risk-takers who, again, tend to be men. A Brotopia culture was created, which celebrated antisocial men who took risks which may not be socially acceptable, and it proliferated in technology. The technology industry then realized it had few women in its ranks and hired recruiters to rectify the situation. Yet, they realized most women found technology ill-suited because of its antisocial, risk-loving culture where they felt ostracized.[163]

WHY DON'T WOMEN STAY IN, OR RETURN TO, TECHNOLOGY CAREERS

Technology is a critical component of business today and is here to stay. In an article called "Six Technology Trends That Will Shape Businesses In 2020," the author Alison Coleman shows businesses that do not keep up with the latest technology trends will be left behind.[164] Since we need to work within the parameters of technology, we must implement solutions.

---

163 Emily Chang, *Brotopia: Breaking up the Boys' Club of Silicon Valley* (New York: Penguin Audio, 2018), Audible audio ed., 37 min.

164 Alison Coleman, "Six Technology Trends That Will Shape Businesses in 2020," *Forbes*, Feb 4, 2020.

In my business, I give a lot of tours to women who are starting over professionally. I find myself in conversations with many women who I define as technology refugees. They have left fields in technology after extensive training and do not wish to return. Looking for a new path, they are physically and emotionally broken. After listening to their stories, while empathizing with them because of my technology background, I have learned a lot.

As technology constantly evolves, work is done in a project-based environment. New innovations are rolled out and scaled back as newer ideas are brought into the market. This means the technology workers operate in a daily world where they focus on a project which is run by a project manager. The goal of the project manager is for the project to run on time, within budget, and according to specifications. Managing these three areas of time, cost, and scope is always challenging.

In technology projects, the scope changes often because of rapidly changing requirements in the industry. To keep up with the technological change, project work demands all team members use effective soft skills. While running a project, a professional must communicate effectively with multiple colleagues to define, start, propel, and compete the project. Everyone must work well with others to achieve the common goal of meeting the project's objective.

Soft skills, which are used on technology projects, matter and should be appreciated because the consequences of hiring individuals without them leads to tricky job situations and repeated personality conflicts with colleagues. When workplace strife arises because of these conflicts, a professional is unable to effectively do the job, causing delayed projects and unmet requirements. The worker ends up stressed out and working longer hours to compensate. They are in a position, company, or industry where there is an employment misfit. Furthermore, negative emotional spillover happens, which as we recall from Chapter One, is when an employee brings work concerns home and is unable to thrive personally.

Eventually, the workers must leave this career path as it does not meet present or future needs of a moral fit. If she works in a culture with the structural inequities of institutional betrayal of the wage gap, sexism, and unconscious bias, her feelings of being a career and moral misfit are perpetuated. She plans her exit and may become a sidepreneur. Our next woman entrepreneur decided to work on a side career while keeping her full-time role using improvisation.

AMY'S AWESOME ANTICS

Amy Westrup, who runs an Applied Improv Program as a sidepreneur, understands how misfits gravitate to comedy, explaining, "The majority of people don't fit in on some level and use humor to neutralize that feeling." She explains in improv, one can fit in if they follow the skills, techniques, and rules to adapt to any situation and create connections. Shortly after becoming an entrepreneur, Amy called to tell me her consulting gig with ComedySportz was going to be featured on the local news.[165] The television news reporter

---

165 "CSZ Applied Improv," Private Events, ComedySportz, accessed January 24, 2021.

wanted to film a news segment at my new business. Thrilled, I was asked to invite some guests to do improv on television so we could share how to help us all celebrate the fun of learning to fit in. I reached out to the nearby University of Wisconsin Milwaukee (UWM) Lubar Entrepreneurship Center (LEC), which was helping me set up and refine the Awesome Women Incubator Model.

I was thrilled when they agreed to attend. During the filming, we learned some improv tricks to help us integrate newcomers into a friendly community setting. A few days after filming and airing of the news segment, I attended a workshop at the UWM LEC, and the leader, Nicole Powley, signaled for me to pay attention to the icebreaking activities which encouraged the group to relax and get along.

ROCK, PAPER, SCISSORS ANYONE?

One such icebreaker is an incredible group bonding experience of Rock, Paper, Scissors. It consists of taking two hundred freshly arrived meeting newcomers to play a quick game with their hands depicting one of the three outcomes. When the newcomer loses, they join in chanting the winner's name. It culminates in a championship match where everyone feels a sense of belonging and friendships form. Creating a culture where everyone fits in makes sense financially, boosts productivity, and allows for full participation. It helps future entrepreneurs feel engaged and supported. This is one example of many types of fun activities Nicole arranges at UWM, a large, urban university.

Companies should pay attention to what the UWM LEC has already implemented. According to Fortune magazine, "managers spend 17 percent of their time, or almost a day a week, supervising poorly performing employees." These poor hiring choices, according to the US Department of Labor, "can cost up to 30 percent of the employee's potential first-year earnings."[166]

Even if someone fits in, they may not feel welcome. According to research by CareerBuilder, the cost of a poor hiring choice was almost $15,000, while that of losing a good hiring choice is $29,600.[167] Employees leave not because the work is too hard, but because they do not feel a part of the community.

The UWM LEC understands that many of the participants in their program may not become business owners; what they focus on is the learning moment of still being part of a team. They let everyone know they still belong and can participate in whichever way they seek to move forward. One such way they assist is through workshops on how to refine a new business idea and document it into the Business Model Canvas.

BUSINESS MODEL CANVAS

When someone starts a business, or imagines its feasibility, they detail the daily operations incessantly with a series of

---

166 David Sturt, "3 Ways to Weed Out a Bad Job Candidate: Don't Make Another Bad Hire Ever Again," *Fortune Insiders (blog)*, *Medium*, September 16, 2013.

167 "Nearly Three in Four Employers Affected by a Bad Hire, According to a Recent CareerBuilder Survey," CareerBuilder press release, December 7, 2017, on the CareerBuilder website, accessed April 4, 2021.

stories about how the business will exist. They ponder who the customer will be, how they will discover the products, and what and how will they purchase. Thankfully, there is a tool which can be found online to consolidate all of this information called the Business Model Canvas.

In 2005, Alexander Osterwalder and Yves Pigneur created the Business Model Canvas.[168] It is used during the initial months of the Tier of Canvasser, as the founder fleshes out her ideas. It can be updated electronically, or on post-it notes, adding and revising many new ideas that change rapidly and require evaluation. Eventually, when the founder seeks funding from a bank or an investor, she can elaborate on the information in the canvas by putting it into a business plan for the financial professional to review. Yet, she will return to and place evolving information in the Business Model Canvas as the business grows.

The canvas can be accessed by doing a quick search online. When filling out the canvas, a business owner succinctly explains and describes her thought process of what needs to be done and outsourced to create value. Subsequently, she lays out the infrastructure, customers, and finances, evaluating them accordingly.

- Desirability of the Product or Service by which customers
    - value proposition
    - customer relationships
    - channels
    - customer segments

---

168 "What is a Business Model?," Strategizer, accessed February 8, 2021.

- Viability of Cost compared to Revenue
  - cost structures
  - revenue streams
- Feasibility of bringing it to the customer
  - key resources
  - key activities
  - partnerships

These categories are visually laid out based on the desirability by customers, viability of what can sell and what it will cost, and how feasible it is to deliver. A framework is established, and the tradeoffs of adding or removing items in each of these categories can be effectively evaluated.[169]

Here is a great example of someone using the Business Model Canvas to thrive and grow. She is in transition and does not know where she fits.

RHONDA'S REINVENTION

Rhonda is in her mid-fifties and is in the process of moving from the initial tier of the Awesome Women model, Discovery, to that of the second tier, called Canvasser. She got divorced a few years ago and is deciding which direction her life should take. Her two kids are in middle school and in high school. She would like to get back into her field of social work but is having trouble getting her license transferred and thus getting hired. Rhonda is in the Awesome Woman Tier of Discovery.

---

169 Ibid.

Rhonda is contemplating starting her own practice, yet she needs to gather energy to begin. Her biggest obstacle is the lack of familial support for this idea, which causes her to doubt her own abilities. Even though Rhonda appears very confident and has an answer to everything, she is lacking networking and support systems, both huge impediments as networking is important in gaining momentum when starting a business. Also, Rhonda seeks accountability.

Rhonda's story is very typical of many women who start a business but decide it is not the right decision. She moved from the Tier of Discovery and dabbled in the Tier of Canvasser. Yet over time, Rhonda loses her self-motivation and becomes depressed. She wants to stop wasting her time. Rhonda decides, with her family's guidance, to go back and work in a setting where she is not the boss. She gets a job, pivots and takes another job, then at long last, finds another job which is a good fit. Happy to have gone back to work and resumed her career, Rhonda is proud of her attempt to launch a business yet would not return, as she needs the steady income.

If Rhonda's story resonates with you as someone who has been contemplating leaving the Tier of Discovery, I would work on defining the Business Model Canvas by looking up the term online and filling out the categories. You can access such a template on my business MalamaDoe's website at my author page.[170]

To move forward, you must decide if you want to officially enter the Tier of Canvasser by naming a company, forming

---

170 "Book by Sheila Long," MalamaDoe, accessed April 7, 2021.

a legal entity, and setting up a bank account. If you do not take these steps, you could still delve into the answers needed on the Business Model Canvas, which is what Rhonda did above. This process of Canvassing is time-consuming, yet the answer you find may lead you to realize your perfect fit.

What Rhonda went through attempting to launch a company reminds me of what my colleague Patty Trinko wishes for, that the "world of work had a coaching or mentor approach." Patty believes that with such an approach, there would be fewer people in fields where they do not fit.

HELPING MISFITS CREATE "REALNESS, MEANING, AND BELONGING AT WORK"

Women who are trailblazers may not fit in at work, and to stop this cycle from perpetuating, we must break it. Our youngest workers are also impacted; they want to contribute and feel they belong. Colleen McFarland writes about how our youngest workers only know a world with cellular phones, thus grow up being tech savvy. She advocates for their need to feel connected to their workplace by having necessary data at their fingertips to make sound decisions. In her book, *Disconnected: How to Use People Data to Deliver Realness, Meaning, and Belonging at Work,* she recommends workplaces house job requirements and needed assistance for workers online where they can access it.[171] This practice helps all workers know what is expected of them and they

---

171 Colleen McFarland, *Disconnected: How to Use People Data to Deliver Realness, Meaning, and Belonging at Work* (Potomac: New Degree Press, 2020).

can feel reassured. Once reassured, they will contribute and stay in the company, fit in, and grow.

For future women employees to feel a sense of belonging, we must accept women with the attributes they bring to the table, pass the Equal Rights Amendment, and face the stigma of past institutional betrayal. To ensure we do not perpetuate the cycle of exclusion of women in existing companies for the next generation, employees must create a culture of change by opening the gates for all, especially women. Here are some ways to provide equal opportunities:

- Ensure women have equal representation and are actively involved in defining job requirements and hiring, interviewing, and promoting industry leaders.
- Provide entrance exams for interested parties and job applicants with accurate success criteria assessed.
- Reward workers who succeed by maintaining job responsibilities, company objectives, and a reasonable workload.
- Implement companywide departmental objectives to celebrate a great job fit, work-life balance, and healthy camaraderie.
- Develop industrywide standards, which foster a feeling of mutual respect, including acknowledging the burden and emotional tax placed on the BIPOC community and women.
- Offer vetted industrywide awards for companies and managers who retain and promote members of the BIPOC community and women.
- Create company cultures which ensure concerns are mentioned, elevated, addressed, and improved upon with regard to sexism and unfair treatment. Ensure supportive

and celebratory actions for the courageous people who raise concerns are recognized companywide and with the press, industry leaders, and at home with families.

By implementing the above actions, the gender inequality which silences and shames women can stop. Furthermore, these issues will be addressed and better understood by all, ensuring more voices speak up and are heard. By creating a more "welcoming atmosphere, instead of an isolating, hostile one" women will not self-select out, but rather will enter, and continue, in fields because they know they belong.[172] We want women to start and plan out the future of their businesses with the Business Model Canvas for the right reasons. We want them to have a path to follow that leads to the perfect job fit.

---

172 Emily Chang, *Brotopia: Breaking up the Boys' Club of Silicon Valley* (New York: Penguin Audio, 2018), Audible audio ed., 1 hr., 21 min.

CHAPTER SEVEN

How Awesome Women Confront Sexism

———

NO HUG NEEDED

"Hey, where's my hug?" I leaned over to distract my two-year-old from touching her baby brother and picked her up. As I looked up, a guest walked in my front door with two similarly aged children. I introduced myself and welcomed her into my home where I was hosting the newcomer toddler playgroup.

With a huge smile, she introduced herself: "My name is Kellie Freeze." It was clear from the first moment we met that Kellie was a lively breath of fresh air. "I just moved back home after living in Chicago. I used to work in television, but because of work-life balance concerns, we are here now." Kellie and I became fast friends.

A few years later, Kellie landed a position as a television critic and excelled in the role, calling it her "dream job." She remembered, "I'd go to LA and interview celebrities. I get to travel abroad and do set visits and then come home. That was really fun."

Things changed when, at a work event, Kellie had a life-changing experience when a celebrity she had interviewed before behaved inappropriately. Instead of answering a question she and her female colleague posed, he made very crude, vulgar statements in her ear. Kellie replied, "Wow, I'm super married."

Undeterred, the celebrity inappropriately touched a horrified and sickened Kellie. He then hugged her while touching her inappropriately for a second time.

After the other female journalist refused a hug from him, saying, "Oh, no thanks. You know, I'm married. I don't really need a hug," the celebrity grabbed her face and kissed her on the mouth.

Kellie ended the "interview" as a male colleague intervened and distracted the celebrity by asking him, "*Hey, where's my hug?*"

After this incident, Kellie second-guessed herself on all of her interactions with interview subjects. She explained, "My job was to ask questions. I'm not supposed to let anything get in the way. While you're interviewing someone, they are your best friend. If I had to sit back and think, 'Am I smiling too much?' then I can't be myself. It just sucked the love out of what I was doing."

Kellie reported the incident to her journalist colleagues, but not to the cable network and not to the police. She explained,

"My job is to have access; I get interviews because I am a great interviewer. Talent loves me. Publicists love me. The networks love me. If I'm a 'problem,' does my access dry up?"

Two years after the incident, and eighteen months after the #MeToo movement became mainstream, Kellie read that the actor had been charged with groping other women and her memories of that night came flooding back. She remembered reading in the comments section of those articles, not "These poor women are victims," but "These women are sluts."

Kellie says that she spent numerous nights crying herself to sleep. She was furious and disappointed in herself for not speaking up. Two and a half years after the incident, Kellie did a very brave thing. She called the Assistant District Attorney and added her name to the list of accusers. She told the Assistant District Attorney,

"Let this woman know I believe her, because I am her. Let her know that, and what's going to happen in the news, in the press, is going to be horrible for her. But I completely support her, and I know I'll never know her name. And she'll probably never know mine. But just let her know that I know, that it happened to her."

The case was going to trial at the time that we sat together for this interview. There are now thirty women who accuse this celebrity of groping. In a separate civil lawsuit, the actor has also been accused of rape.

After I subdued my shock, horror, and sadness, she sympathized with me, "You know, he is a serial sexual offender. You think it could be some like monster-y troll who lives under a bridge." We shook our heads, but he is not. Kellie knew women were treated differently because of their gender, yet the experience "killed my dream a little bit."

Kellie left her job and has now started over in a completely different field. She does not think she will ever return to television. "I miss my people. I miss that camaraderie. I love television. But, sometimes money isn't the be-all, end-all, either. Your happiness is more important."

If only someone had advocated for Kellie when it happened, this would have turned out differently. Her career would have continued, and countless victims would have been spared. The role of institutional sexism in the industry, and the subsequent institutional betrayal that resulted from it, played a part in creating the daily reality for those who witnessed this permissible behavior.

What was needed in the industry for this story, and that of countless others to never have happened, is the critical role of courage. It was what the researcher who coined the term institutional betrayal, Jennifer Freyd, calls institutional courage.

"**Institutional courage** is the antidote to institutional betrayal. It includes institutional accountability and transparency, as when institutions respond well to disclosures and when institutions conduct anonymous surveys of victimization within the institution and then use the data to become healthier."[173]

When reeling from the aftermath of betrayal, each survivor brings their courage to the table. In this book, I state objectives and give strategies by presenting real people who faced real situations. By hearing these stories, I hope you are compelled to create incredible opportunities for yourself and others with your own courage.

NETWORKING GONE WRONG

When I was disconnected in my world professionally after relocating, I knew networking would be difficult. Since my field, STEM, has many more men than women, navigating this gender inequality as a woman attending any networking event is always tricky. Also, I had a small network locally and knew no women who would attend STEM events with me.

---

173 Jennifer J. Freyd, PhD, "Research," accessed February 6, 2021.

I had two experiences with leaders in local organizations where, because of my gender, no one knew what to do. At one event, I knew a leader personally and when dealing with him previously in groups, his continual eagerness to approach me and failure to complete sentences when we conversed led me to believe he found me attractive. As I debated about attending an event where he spoke, I was reading *Lean In: Women, Work, and the Will to Lead*, a book written by CEO Sheryl Sandberg which encourages women to show up and sit at the table.[174] Realizing few men would second-guess showing up for a key information session because of their gender, I determined I needed to be at the meeting as it offered an important career growth opportunity for me. As I knew his wife much more than the man, I planned to talk over my professional ideas and questions with her.

I attended the meeting, and unfortunately, it was obvious that this man found me attractive when he again he could not complete his sentences. Mortified because of the awkward situation and its impact on my future career, I left immediately following the meeting. Thankfully, days later, I bumped into the man's wife only to find out she was furious I had attended this meeting in my former field.

Soon afterward, I attended another event and was brushed off by a different male leader. The unprofessionalism toward me in both of these experiences made it clear I was in a no-win situation. Although these two groups hosting the meetings had made a great effort for attendees to build relationships

174 Sheryl Sandberg, *Lean In: Women, Work and the Will to Lead* (New York: Knopf, 2013).

and feel they belonged, the underlying microaggressions were still present. I realized how when a woman feels awkward and like a misfit, there was a clear signal of who was, and who was not, welcome.

In addition to the awkward gender inequality in STEM, I knew I would face long hours and high stress in a field where I did not feel I belonged and would not be rewarded for staying. Sadly, the best strategy was to not return to the technology industry. The time and place was not for me. I knew I could find a better fit aligned with my morals. I took the steps to put the building blocks in place to start my own business.

A CONSTANT COMPANION AS WE GROW OUR BUSINESS

What I did by leaving the field of technology was courageous. I set boundaries to ensure my needs were met, prioritized, and addressed, which is very important for women business owners. Another important matter is the critical role of networking. Below are steps women running businesses pass through in the Awesome Women Incubator Model, described in depth in Chapter Two. As a woman's business grows, networking and selling requirements in each tier vary, yet each tier requires healthy relationships with men and women.

- In Discovery, an owner determines which market to enter.
- In Canvassing, an owner decides how things get done.
- In Growth, an owner gains customers.
- In Prosperer, an owner assists existing clients.
- In Fulfillment, an owner networks with colleagues.
- In Expansion, an owner breaks into new markets.

If unhealthy, sexist situations occur at any tier, women's businesses risk the chance of not progressing or, in the worst case, not surviving at all. To survive by networking, a business owner must address sexism caused by gender inequality. Sadly, women running businesses often attend events alone without someone watching their back. Thankfully, I had a wonderful person watching my back as I launched my business.

TOM THE ULTIMATE NETWORKER

Having worked in sales for over a decade, I witnessed many people who had an incredible ability to forge relationships through networking. They put people at ease, listened to their stories, and built incredible partnerships by creating authentic friendships. When I think of networking, I will always remember my friend Thomas P. Leisle, Jr. He was, hands down, the best networker I ever met.

First of all, Tom always acted and dressed like a true professional. A few months after the Grand Opening of Malama-Doe, I knew Tom, who had devoted at least fifteen years of his life to inviting people to events so they could make great connections and build a better future, was needed. He would be the perfect host at an event celebrated in and outside of my workplace, the annual Tour of America's Dairyland Shorewood Criterium Cycling Classic. This professional bike race took place a few hours on a weekday evening in June, outside MalamaDoe's front door, normally next to a vibrant, bustling sidewalk which would be converted with the arrival of "the largest competitive road cycling series in the US."[175] A par-

---

[175] "Schedule," Tour of America's Dairyland, accessed March 25, 2021.

ty-like atmosphere would arrive on our sidewalk, which was an excellent opportunity for the women-owned businesses at MalamaDoe to network and grow sales.

Tom readily accepted the opportunity to attend. He became the perfect host greeting guests who entered the event, making needed introductions, and staying until everyone was comfortable. He would do this while drinks and appetizers were consumed, and cowbells were rung to cheer on the cyclists speeding past. Tom would gauge the interest of the visitor, never tolerating the existence of a sexist culture, yet finding a common discussion point with them. Afterwards, he would find a new person and connect them.

So that night, as I gave tours of my facility to interested parties, Tom was right in the middle of it all as the first attendee to arrive and the last one to leave—he knew how to help women thrive in a networking environment. Tom would follow up with everyone the next day to ensure all went well, and if his calendar allowed, he would talk to them about future networking events. **Tom would continue that cycle day after day, tirelessly.** Tom truly wanted to see people succeed professionally. He was a huge supporter of women in business.

THE BUSINESS JOURNAL MENTORING MONDAY EVENT

I have found that many women do not have the luxury to exit a field where they feel uncomfortable. If they experience awkward events around others who support them, they can collectively plan to use tactics to stop inappropriate comments and behavior. However, when they are alone at a business event, owning the outcome is tough.

*"**Sexism** is the result of assumptions, misconceptions, and stereotypes that rationalize discrimination, mistreatment, and objectification of people based on their sex, gender, or sexual orientation."*

CATALYST [176]

Sexism, and how an organization or industry deals with it, matters. Vulnerable women, especially those who lack a powerful network, fall prey. Women in uncommitted relationships are especially at risk if a sexist culture is running rampant. Also, when women move into positions of leadership and evolve professionally, they witness sexism in the workplace and its proliferation threatens to stifle their career and those who they are there to protect.

One way to combat sexism in the workplace is through Institutional Courage. One such organization which is leading the charge on this front is the American City Business Journals through the incredible annual Mentoring Monday. It is an event for women and takes place at the beginning of each new calendar year nationwide. Aspiring women meet with established local leaders at the annual Mentoring Monday.

176 Negin Sattari, Emily Shaffer, PhD., Sarah DiMuccio, and Dnika J. Travis, PhD., "Interrupting Sexism at Work: What Drives Men to Respond Directly or Do Nothing?," *Catalyst*, June 25, 2020, accessed April 5, 2021.

Everyone works toward the common goal of "facilitat(ing) women's leadership development by connecting those leaders with up-and-coming professionals one-on-one."[177]

I have either sponsored or attended this event annually to grow my business for the last few years. As an observer, I sit in on conversations, knowing the same question will inevitably be asked. When I hear it, I take a deep breath as it always comes from a young, accomplished, attractive woman.

She asks the mentor, "I work with all men. Well, all of the bosses are men, and when I ask them for advice, or to be my mentor, they think I am hitting on them."

"We understand," the mentors reply.

She continues, "What can I do to let them know that I am working on my career, and I am not interested in them, other than professionally?"

Every time I hear it, I sit there infuriated. I think to myself, *"You have got to be kidding me. How can we have women move into roles with more responsibility if leaders are so self-centered?"*

I am reminded of a famous quote from the year 1837. Feminist activist Sarah Grimke said, *"But I ask no favors for my sex. I surrender not our claim to equality. All I ask of our brethren is, that they will take their feet from off our necks."*[178]

177 Mark Kass, "Speed Coaching — Mentoring Monday Draws Big Crowd: Slideshow," *Milwaukee Business Journal,* updated on April 3, 2017, accessed January 18, 2020.

178 Mikkelson, David, "Did These Words Originate with Ruth Bader Ginsberg?," Fact Check, *Snopes,* September 24, 2020, accessed March 6, 2021.

STOPPING UNWANTED ADVANCES

When I delve into how to handle this situation, I find a great article from *Forbes* online called, "When the Boss Hits on You." Also, I find question after question posted on the internet from workers in the same boat. Based on this article, there are no legal repercussions an employee can take when her boss hits on her. Also, human resources is powerless in these situations. The article recommends having a man pick you up from work. It also recommends talking about a significant other when the man in power hits on you. One suggestion is to have a clear, respectful conversation with the person doing you harm.[179] None of these scenarios on how to address this abuse of power are acceptable.

Some believe women lack confidence to stand up to their abusers. Any woman who is being sexually harassed by the person who handles her employment, pay, and promotion ability should not be put in the awkward situation of confronting the inappropriate behavior head on. In this situation where there is an abuse of power, the woman is naturally fearful. In no way, shape, or form does it denote a lack of confidence. On the contrary, it represents a failed system of equality for women.

I am reminded of a famous quote from Supreme Court Justice Ruth Bader Ginsburg: *"The pedestal upon which women have been placed has all too often, upon closer inspection, been revealed as a cage."*[180]

179 Susan Adams, "When the Boss Hits on You," *Forbes*, June 25, 2013.
180 "Ruth Bader Ginsburg in Pictures and Her Own Words," *BBC News*, September 19, 2020, accessed January 16, 2020.

I challenge the reader to speak up about sexism when you see it. This next story should give you some inspiration.

PUTTING AN END TO IT

While researching more constructive solutions, I found an article entitled, "Interrupting Sexism at Work." It is from Catalyst, based on a study conducted with almost 1,500 men, and evaluates why men do and do not "take action to interrupt workplace sexism."[181] Their findings are noteworthy and seem to be ones that will prove effective.

The report reads that for sexism to stop, what needs to happen is that a man needs to speak up. Why a man, you may ask? For some odd reason, a woman's efforts will not go very far, but a man will be heard loud and clear. According to this study, men need to voice their concern because they have more positions of leadership and thus know more leaders with power in the organization.

"Men more **committed** to dismantling sexism, **confident** in their ability to interrupt, **aware** of the positive benefits of interrupting, and invested in the **impact** on the

---

181 Negin Sattari, Emily Shaffer, PhD., Sarah DiMuccio, and Dnika J. Travis, PhD., "Interrupting Sexism at Work: What Drives Men to Respond Directly or Do Nothing?," *Catalyst*, June 25, 2020, accessed April 5, 2021.

common good are more likely to directly
interrupt sexism."

CATALYST[182]

The culture of the organization is also important. If this type of setting is one where all "feel valued, trusted, authentic, and psychologically safe," the likelihood of having a man interrupt the behavior increases.

"Organizational climates perceived by men to be more **silencing**, **combative**, and **futile** are associated with doing nothing in response to sexism."

CATALYST[183]

STOP STIFLING SUZANNE

I met Suzanne in 2015 and was impressed as she ran her own business in an "all-female circle." Years later, Suzanne became a commercial real estate advisor, moving from an "all-female circle" to an "all-male circle."

---

182 Ibid.
183 Ibid.

Going to an office where she was the only woman was an adjustment. She was in a "competitive and aggressive" culture. She learned to check in with herself and knew when something was off, it may have been because she had different wiring. Unfortunately, she encountered problems with her colleagues in the office.

"I would do so well, and then," she paused, embarrassed, "I get hit on."

She added, "I went to the executive director directly. He was really upset when he heard it."

The executive director held a meeting without Suzanne and told her fellow advisors, "We're gonna talk about sexual harassment. We don't tolerate that."

Suzanne was relieved and told me, "And it stopped." She was happy she brought it up, and happier that her boss addressed it immediately. She said, "Why should I leave the job? I love what I do, and I've worked hard to get here."

Thankfully, this manager knew what he was doing, and Suzanne stood up for herself. I applaud him for his Institutional Courage.

MENTORING AND ETHICS TRAINING

Looking back on what Suzanne, the mentees, and myself experienced, I see themes emerging which can be remedied with prioritizing basic business ethics. Here are some ways to put an end to it.

First, men need to accept they have an easier road networking and do not suffer the repercussions women do. Second, leaders need to prioritize mentoring women and focus on their talents. They need to develop social skills when working with attractive women, which includes checking their ego. Most importantly, leaders need to make the rollout and training of basic business ethics mandatory. They then need to follow it up with quality intervention when they see poor, unethical choices being made.

With increased training, colleagues can support women by having a more educated viewpoint. Also, everyone can acknowledge the difficulty of being the sole woman anywhere. Hopefully, we will recognize women who are lacking in support and demonstrate compassion. Then, and only then, we can celebrate when a woman walks into the room and raises her voice.

If there ever was a story that made this more evident, it is our next one.

JEAN'S CAREER AS AN ARTISTS' REP

While writing this book, Jean Grow was introduced to me because she created a neighborhood book club to talk about racism. Jean had recently taken advantage of an early retirement offer after a twenty-year career as a professor and, in the last year, co-director of Marquette University's Institute for Women's Leadership. I was excited to get to meet Jean, who was pivoting to diversity, equity, and inclusion work, focused on the advertising industry where she had some unfinished business. As she experienced roadblocks because she is a woman, Jean aims to create a different scenario.

In the 1980s, Jean entered the established, male-dominated advertising world selling artists' photography, film, and illustration to advertising agencies. She grew her business with illustrators on both coasts, providing access to the Midwest market, while based out of Chicago. She recalled, "Literally every single client that I ever had, every art director or creative director who I ever worked with, was a white male." Jean recalled when dealing with men in the advertising industry, she normalized the unspoken rules about some "inappropriate behavior."

Although this behavior clearly did not extend to all her clients, Jean persevered and continued to build her business. She didn't want to listen to people who told her she shouldn't try and that all of the work should go to the men. Jean knew people with great talent with whom she would work. Her unpleasant experiences dealing with some men were not uncommon. She decided she would just have to deal with it when men tried to grab her and make sure they didn't: "Why didn't I have the right to get that business as much as anybody else?"

A key client for Jean was a design firm, responsible for roughly 30 to 40 percent of her business. Jean worked with one of the partners who was a very "famous" designer. She recalled, "He was kind of known to be a lecherous human. He was always, always grabbing (someone), everybody knew what he did. That's the other thing, like this stuff is not shocking, it is 'normal.'"

She had worked with this client for about four years, and he gave her a lot of work: "He was my best client. And over the years I had learned how to handle him. I knew where to stand in a room so that I could protect myself. I always knew where the doors were. I knew when to end the conversation. I learned how to manage dealing with him when I had to deal with him, and still get work out of him."

One day, Jean met him for lunch, and, at the end of lunch, he put a hotel room key on the table between their two cups of coffee. She sat there stunned: "It was really a depressing moment."

When she saw the key, Jean knew she had to walk away from the business, four years of work, which she had so diligently built. She recalled, "Obviously in that moment, you realize that you have to make a decision. So, obviously, I got up and walked away."

After the depression and shock wore off, Jean was furious. She never dealt with this client or his company again. "He never called to give me work again and then, you know, it was pointless for me to pursue it. There are unspoken rules and I, I knew full well what the next step was if I wanted more work."

Jean had been groomed by this man, or possibly by the industry. Not only Jean was groomed, but so was her family. He had "pretended to be friends with my husband as well. We knew his family, and the children." Jean knows the behavior she had to tolerate then still goes on, though it is less common.

JEAN'S DEFENSE IN DEFENSE OF WOMEN

A year later, Jean closed up her business and moved from Chicago, taking a corporate job in another state. A few years later, she pursued her PhD in mass communication and her research agenda always focused on diversity, equity, and inclusion. Her last big project focused on interviewing critical women and men who were instrumental in the Time's Up revelations in the advertising industry.

Jean explained her feelings about what women often have to tolerate in the workplace being rooted in sexism:

"It is not about being inappropriate and they would only do it with people they don't know. This whole idea that it's always a woman's fault or you look some way, or they would not have done it if they had known your family. That is the biggest lie. These acts are assaults, they're acts of power and assault against women. It is not because you look good or you're attracting them. It's like blaming women for rape because they wear short dresses."

As a professor, Jean challenged her students to see the world of advertising more honestly. For some, that was a welcome message. They describe Jean as one who "makes a lasting impact on your life" and others who use such incredible words as dedicated, passionate, motivational, honest, and inspirational. One even called her a "rare jewel." I can sure see why.

Jean is now the founder and chief truth teller at Grow, a DEI (Diversity, Equity, and Inclusion) consultancy found online under her name, Jean Grow. As Grow targets small to midsize advertising agencies and marketing firms, she continues to fight for equity for women as she pushes for increased diversity and inclusion across the industry. Jean is one of our heroes.

NEXT STEPS AS WE CELEBRATE FEMININITY
We need to have women build businesses by celebrating, not minimizing, what they bring to the table. When we promote our independence and leadership, we celebrate our courage and values. We do it when, as author Jerramy Fine explains, it is done in service to others.

"Most of us would agree that dismissing someone purely because she is female is unacceptable. Yet dismissing feminine qualities and feminine

expression (including princess
culture) is still widely condoned."

AUTHOR JERRAMY FINE, *IN DEFENSE OF THE
PRINCESS: HOW PLASTIC TIARAS AND FAIRYTALE
DREAMS CAN INSPIRE SMART, STRONG WOMEN*[184]

Let's do our part to offer our assistance to women. In this
chapter, we heard the stories of women who use their voice
to speak up against the injustices. They are the heroes among
us who launch, plan, and attend women's groups, conferences, and mentoring events, such as the Business Journal's
Mentoring Monday. The microcosms of support for women
allows us to further move the needle for women's equity and
enlighten women about starting new conversations.

We must realize that there are women unable to voice their
concerns. We know they do not receive interviews, mentoring, or promotions at work because of their gender
and witness when they exit promising careers. Let's stand
alongside the decent people who defend women's voices.
Our actions ensure women can be listened to, now and for
future generations.

To stop sexism while networking, we need to speak up,
especially in industries where there is a gender imbalance.
We need to understand that no one knows what to do. Yet,

---

184 Jerramy Fine, *In Defense of the Princess: How Plastic Tiaras and Fairytale
Dreams Can Inspire Smart, Strong Women* (Philadelphia: Running Press
Adult, 2016), 202.

when we as leaders listen to the stories, we can reevaluate and rectify priorities. We must lend an ear when someone starts over professionally and become an ally. We must give our support for those courageous enough to speak up in the face of injustice. We must celebrate women whose actions are overtly feminine and ensure they do not suffer negative repercussions for doing so.

Finally, we must promote the companies that are leading the way, offering training on ethical women's mentoring and marketing themselves as fair places for women to work. More information can be found on my business MalamaDoe's website at my author page. Let's build workplaces where someone can be different from the norm and be rewarded for it. We want a workplace which is "safe, fair, and dignified for women of all kinds."[185]

---

185 "About," Times Up, accessed March 25, 2021.

PART THREE

BREAKING THE MOLD

CHAPTER EIGHT

Combatting the Macro Effects of Microaggression

―――

CINDY'S TRUTHS ON SCALING A BUSINESS

"Being smart is not always the popular place to be." Cindy Machles, who we met in Chapter Four when she left her employer to create Glue Advertising, remembers some tough high school years.[186] Cindy stood out in school and felt conflicted about it. "I didn't wake up one day with a ton of confidence, I had to gain it. I had to get to a place where I felt really good about my intellect. Then, I knew it was going to take me places."

With time and experience, Cindy became comfortable with her inner workings, becoming a brilliant consumer and packaged goods marketer. In her current role as the chief executive officer of Glue Advertising, she built a company that offers hands-on, streamlined advertising services which

---

186 "About," Glue Advertising, accessed February 18, 2021.

value each employee's intellect. She has learned to delegate and embraced having her business associates work alongside others with complementary skill sets so they can "row the boat in the same direction."

She had the business acumen, knowledge, and commitment. Yet, she was not immune to compromised feelings about financial risk. For the first few years after launching Glue, she tossed and turned nightly about her finances. Yet, she did not fear failure because it was not an option.

"I started this once I had two kids in college. Failure would have meant pulling one of them out of college. I couldn't fail. If there could potentially be a fire, I always seem to be able to make it work. It is critical I am confident in my ability to do that. For me, seeing the goal line and figuring out how to get there is key, and it's not linear. It's staying committed to realizing a vision and changing it as I go."

CINDY MACHLES, CHIEF EXECUTIVE
OFFICER OF GLUE ADVERTISING

Cindy built her company, Glue, into a top-twenty New York City advertising and public relations agency which has been recognized as such since 2015.[187] In 2020, Glue was categorized as one of the top four of over 1,200 competitors, as a featured pick.[188] Glue prides itself in offering best-in-class services through a flat hierarchical structure which delivers clients consistent, high-quality creative and strategic thinking, providing senior level oversight.

Cindy has been a contributor to the book *Founded by Women: Inspiration and Advice from over 100 Female Founders* and is a solicited speaker to educate about personal branding as a driver of growth.[189] As far as Glue's potential, Cindy sees it as exiting the Tier of Growth and expanding through strategic partnerships with the right cultural fit. Cindy is committed to achieving growth, expansion, and staying ahead of the trend with continual reinvention. We know she will make it happen.

CORPORATE CULTURE TRANSFORMATION AND MARGARITA'S WOMEN DIGNITY ALLIANCE

One way to grow a company is to build upon established policies and reposition them to enable women's business growth. Our next three leaders are tasked with helping reposition or transform corporate values to enhance women as valued

187 "Cindy Machles," Contributors, Founded by Women, accessed February 20, 2021.

188 "We Scored 1,214 Advertising Agencies in New York, NY and Picked the Top 36," Business Services, Expertise, accessed February 19, 2021.

189 Cindy Machles et al, "Cindy Machles," *Founded by Women: Inspiration and Advice from over 100 Female Founders* (San Francisco: Databird Business Journal, 2021), 109-114, downloadable pdf.

talent in the organization. Each of them plays a critical role in reshaping the future. Our first leader, Margarita Pineda-Ucero, rose to the top ranks of corporate America and now devotes her life to giving back. She wants to ensure women are treated with dignity. She is changing the narrative with encouraging companies to have Institutional Courage.

The first part of Margarita Pineda-Ucero's career was as a corporate executive in the international financial industry. She moved internationally, traveled extensively, and worked in a continually fast-paced environment. In her role as a C-Suite executive, she was tasked with making challenging choices which would impact many people's work and home lives. She relied on her faith to handle the consistently high demands, pressure, and level of stress of her role.

After successfully completing her assignment at GE Capital as chief risk officer for the Latin America region, Margarita formed Women Dignity Alliance. She wanted it to be a platform where women and their corporations could converse and women could be "valued, included, and considered relevant to the overall success of the business." She became a storyteller through her talks and workshops.

"I give a unique perspective on life experiences and challenges that women in the workplace consistently face, and the courageous choices that they have to make, when

moving along in life and in their professional careers, being single, or wives, or
daughters and caring for parents, or mothers, or community leaders and more."

MARGARITA PINEDA-UCERO, WOMEN DIGNITY ALLIANCE[190]

As a consultant, advisor, and board director, her approach is "to enhance diversity and inclusion with efficiency and productivity." Margarita conducts strategic and operational transformations while enhancing corporate culture. She also provides resources to nonprofits dedicated to helping women in life crisis situations, in professional development, and to career women when they are at a crossroads balancing personal life challenges.[191]

DAVE ON MAKING CORPORATE CHANGES MORE INCLUSIVE & REPORTING HARASSMENT

One company implementing improvements in this area of Institutional Courage is Rockwell Automation. I met a champion of this effort in Dave Vasko when we were in an eight-week course, put on by the YWCA of Southeast Wisconsin, called Unlearning Racism. He is a director of research and development at Rockwell Automation and an executive who is thoughtful and intentional about being an ally for women, as well as the BIPOC community. At Rockwell, he explained,

190 "Our Founder," Women Dignity Alliance, accessed February 16, 2021.
191 Ibid.

"We basically have a culture of integrity, inclusion, and diversity, and that drives matters."

Dave is a big supporter of strong ethics being pushed from the top. He recalls an award the CEO gives out annually for global integrity champions and explained, "This past year, it was won by two bystanders who witnessed sexual harassment." These two people, both in separate instances, felt comfortable reporting the behavior and actions were subsequently taken. Because it supports the company's values, they knew they could not remain silent.

"Ethical accountability from the top down inspires employees to take action, and that drives positive behavior," said Vasko. "Additionally, since it's not an easy thing to do, people are recognized for the positive-driving actions they take, and that drives value."

Our next featured woman has been a corporate executive as well as a candidate for governor. She is doing her part to instill Institutional Courage.

BUILDING BRAVE

After running unsuccessfully to become the governor of Wisconsin against the incumbent, Scott Walker, Mary Burke saw an unmet need for women to build Institutional Courage inside companies. She realized women needed to "access guidance, advice, and perspectives" at their fingertips when the time was right for them. Mary created a woman's resource in Building Brave, a company and app, to respect a woman's limited spare time with the overarching goal of uniting women online. She aims to "break down barriers for women to share guidance, encouragement and inspiration while giving organizations a way to attract, retain and advance women at scale."[192]

OWNING OUR PATH FORWARD BY UNDERSTANDING MICROAGGRESSIONS

The best way we can help women is to recognize when microaggressions occur. In 2019, during Women's Entrepreneurship Week, I hosted a meeting educating women on the work of Dr. Tanya Menon, whose talk on "You Are a Threat—Own It" I discussed in Chapter Five. With her permission, I compiled her content, as well as the below, with the help of my intern Melissa Lieberthal for the attendees.

Microaggressions are "a statement, action, or incident regarded as an instance of indirect, subtle, or unintentional discrimination against members of a marginalized group such as a racial or ethnic minority."[193]

OXFORD DICTIONARY

The most common types, based on the article "15 Microaggressions Women Face On A Daily Basis" on *Bustle* being:

---

192 "Home," Building Brave, accessed February 16, 2021.
193 *Oxford University Press*, s.v. "Microaggression," accessed February 18, 2021.

- Sexist Language
- Sexual Harassment
- Slut Shaming
- Victim Blaming
- Tone Policing
- Language Policing
- Mansplaining
- Sizeism
- Mom Shaming
- Period Shaming
- Stereotypes
- Objectification
- The Wage Gap
- Implicit Bias
- Gaslighting[194]

I surveyed the twenty-two women who attended the event and found over 80 percent experienced sexist language, stereotypes, and mansplaining, and it did not surprise me, as these types of discrimination are mainstream components of our society. Our next featured woman has had so many of the above microaggressions hurled at her, yet she continues to move the needle for equity.

ALEXANDRIA OCASIO-CORTEZ'S START WITH THE GIRL SCOUTS

At age twelve, Girl Scout Alexandria Ocasio-Cortez (AOC) petitioned the Yorktown town board, a suburb of New York

---

194 Susannah Weiss, "15 Microaggressions Women Face On A Daily Basis," *Bustle*, October 26, 2016.

City, to place an aerator into a local pond to make it frog friendly. Her attempt failed yet opened her eyes about how to make an impact.[195] She evolved, finding her strength in her father, a small business owner and architect, who challenged her to be courageous and to not settle for the status quo.[196] Sadly, he left this world too early. She said goodbye to him before leaving for her second year of college in his hospital room, where he courageously battled lung cancer. He died less than a month later in September 2008. His last words to her were "Make me proud."[197] [198]

AOC has made him proud, devoting her life to advocating for policies to ensure communities thrive.[199] In the two years after his death, she interned for US Congressional Representative Ted Kennedy and studied in Niger while on a maternity clinic rotation.[200] [201] After graduating cum laude from Boston University with economics and international relations

---

195 Michelle Ruiz, "AOC's Next Four Years," *Vanity Fair*, October 28, 2020, accessed April 5, 2021.

196 McKenzie Jean-Philippe, "4 Quick Facts to Know about Alexandria Ocasio-Cortez," *Oprah Daily,* August 19, 2020.

197 Michelle Ruiz, "AOC's Next Four Years," *Vanity Fair*, October 28, 2020, accessed April 5, 2021.

198 McKenzie Jean-Philippe, "4 Quick Facts to Know about Alexandria Ocasio-Cortez," *Oprah Daily,* August 19, 2020.

199 Charlotte Alter, "'Change Is Closer Than We Think.' Inside Alexandria Ocasio-Cortez's Unlikely Rise," *Time*, March 21, 2019, accessed February 20, 2021.

200 Andrew Steward, "How Long Was Alexandria Ocasio-Cortez Planning Her Run for Public Office?," *Washington Babylon* (blog), August 28, 2018, accessed February 20, 2021.

201 Eliza Reitman, "The Truth about Alexandria Ocasio-Cortez: The Inside Story of How, in Just One Year, Sandy the Bartender Became a Lawmaker Who Triggers Both Parties," *Insider (blog),* January 6, 2019, accessed February 20, 2021.

degrees, she founded Brook Avenue Press.[202] [203] Her goal was to help promote books that positively depicted the Bronx.[204]

AOC became a business owner again a few years later when she announced her candidacy for the US House of Representatives. She entered the Tier of Canvasser and planned her campaign and signature collection strategy. She then entered the Tier of Growth to raise funds, forge partnerships, and increase awareness for her candidacy. After defeating the incumbent in the 2018 primary, AOC entered the Tier of Prosperer and later the Tier of Fulfillment when she officially won the seat in the US Congress's House of Representatives.[205]

WOMEN ELECTED TO CONGRESS INSPIRE US TO STAND UP TO RESISTANCE

What AOC did by being elected to the US Congress was a critical piece of moving the needle in terms of women's empowerment. She was not alone. The number of voting women members of Congress had grown from eighteen in the ninety-sixth Congress of 1979-1980, increasing every year to the 116th Congress of 2019-2020 with women's representation being 127. That year's 2018 midterm year election was

202 Michelle Ruiz, "AOC's Next Four Years," *Vanity Fair*, October 28, 2020, accessed April 5, 2021.

203 "Biography," About, Congresswoman Alexandria Cortez, accessed April 5, 2021.

204 Daniel Beekman, "Diverse Group of Startups Thriving at City-Sponsored Sunshine Bronx Business Incubator in Hunts Point," *New York Daily News*, July 17, 2012, accessed April 5, 2021.

205 "Speaker Profile Alexandria Ocasio-Cortez," Netroots Nation, accessed February 18, 2021.

significant in the history books because women's empowerment was under attack.

After Hillary Clinton lost the election for the US presidency
to Donald Trump, the subsequent microaggressions toward
women and the BIPOC community were everywhere. Women
stood up for themselves, courageously starting businesses by
running for office. Consequently, the 116th Congress of 2019-
2020 elected 117 women congressional members. It was a
noteworthy increase from 1992, the other Year of the Women
when an incredible number of women, twenty-eight, were
elected.[206] [207]

As women were placed in positions of leadership, especially in
elected roles in government, women's empowerment evolved.
There was a mind shift from rage and depression to that of
collective action on a Ladder of Empowerment. Women
resisted the signs of oppression.[208]

As women moved into positions of power, Tactics of Resistance were on full display by those who did not appreciate
their voice being heard. Paul Kivel breaks them out in his
book, *Uprooting Racism*. As perpetrators

---

206 Dan Murphy, "Ocasio-Cortez Not Proud of Westchester Roots," *Yonkers
Times*, July 18, 2018, accessed February 18, 2021.

207 Jennifer E. Manning and Ida A. Brudnick, "Appendix. Total Number of
Women Who Served in Each Congress," *Women in Congress - Statistics
and Brief Overview, R43244 Version 30* (Washington DC: Congressional
Research Service, updated December 4, 2020), 18, accessed February 19,
2021.

208 Li Zhou, "A Historic New Congress Will Be Sworn in Today," *Vox*, January 3, 2019, accessed February 18, 2021.

1. deny their responsibility as they are "not at fault or responsible"
2. minimize the damage of what is happening as "it is not that bad"
3. blame the victim for being "too emotional"
4. claim they did not intend to damage anything because "it was only a joke"
5. put the actions in the past saying "feminism has gone too far"
6. play the victim and claim women "really have all the power"[209]

In 2019, these characteristics were present when AOC and other members of the BIPOC community took office.

MICROAGGRESSIONS TOWARD AOC AND OTHERS IN CONGRESS

In the 116th Congress, AOC joined the first women Native American Representatives, Deb Haaland and Sharice Davids, and Muslim Representatives Rashida Tlaib and Ilhan Omar.[210] She joined forces with the latter two, Representatives Tlaib and Omar, and added African American Representative Ayanna Pressley, forming The Squad which advocates for "shared humanity."[211]

---

209 Kenneth Jones and Tema Okun, "Ladder of Empowerment," in *Dismantling Racism 2016 Workbook* (Durham: dR works, 2016), 27.

210 Paul Kivel, *White People's Resistance, Uprooting Racism - 4th Edition: How White People Can Work for Racial Justice* (Gabriola Island: New Society Publishers, 2017), 40-46.

211 Li Zhou, "A Historic New Congress Will Be Sworn in Today," *Vox*, January 3, 2019, accessed February 18, 2021.

Since the 2018 election, AOC, The Squad, and other female members of Congress have witnessed the mainstream denial of their accomplishments, minimization of the death threats, and blame of the name calling. For example, in January 2019, after AOC became the youngest woman sworn into the US Congress, *Time* magazine playfully called her "Wonder Woman of the left, Wicked Witch of the right."[212] In late 2020, AOC was called the derogatory terms of "crazy," "disgusting," and two expletives by a fellow congressman, Florida Representative Ted Yoho, on her way to vote.[213]

AOC had grown in her journey advocating for policies to ensure communities thrived and she exemplified the Tier of Expansion. She used her voice to denounce Yoho's and the mainstream actions against all women by inviting other female elected officials to share their similar stories on the House floor. But first, she made her now famous "I am Someone's Daughter" speech, launching a worldwide "viral condemnation of sexism."[214]

In doing so, AOC stood up for the rights of the women, all while the tactics of resistance of denial, minimization, and blame by the offenders were on full display.[215] She collec-

---

212 Wyatte Grantham-Phillips and Jessica Flores, "'The Squad' Stays Strong: Alexandria Ocasio-Cortez, Ilhan Omar, Ayanna Pressley and Rashida Tlaib Win Reelection," *USA Today,* November 4, 2020, accessed February 18, 2021.

213 Charlotte Alter, "'Change Is Closer Than We Think.' Inside Alexandria Ocasio-Cortez's Unlikely Rise," *Time,* March 21, 2019, accessed February 20, 2021.

214 Michelle Ruiz, "AOC's Next Four Years," *Vanity Fair,* October 28, 2020, accessed April 5, 2021.

215 Luke Broadwater and Catie Edmondson, "A.O.C. Unleashes a Viral Condemnation of Sexism in Congress," *New York Times,* July 23, 2020, accessed February 20, 2021.

tively changed the narrative for how microaggressions are addressed with the male US House Majority Leader Representative Steny Hoyer, changing his former support of the apology given by Yoho to then calling it woefully inadequate after actively listening to the stories on the US House floor.[216] [217] As a nation, we see his example as one of how to better understand the collective action required on the Ladder of Empowerment for women.[218]

Yet, less than a year later, as AOC and others worked near the US Capitol on January 6, 2021, rioters launched a violent attack, and again AOC feared for her safety.[219] She knew not only the rioters, but fellow colleagues in Congress, might disclose her whereabouts if she went to the "safe location" where members of Congress were directed to hide. She was physically unharmed that day but again was courageous enough to reveal her status as an assault survivor, again giving voice to the unheard.[220] [221]

216 Paul Kivel, *White People's Resistance, Uprooting Racism - 4th Edition: How White People Can Work for Racial Justice* (Gabriola Island: New Society Publishers, 2017), 40-46.

217 Luke Broadwater and Catie Edmondson, "A.O.C. Unleashes a Viral Condemnation of Sexism in Congress," *New York Times*, July 23, 2020, accessed February 20, 2021.

218 Kenneth Jones and Tema Okun, "Ladder of Empowerment," in *Dismantling Racism 2016 Workbook* (Durham: dR works, 2016), 27.

219 Sarah Ruiz-Grossman, "Alexandria Ocasio-Cortez Recounts Fear That She Was 'Going to Die' in Capitol Attack," *HuffPost* (blog), February 1, 2021, accessed April 5, 2021.

220 Kenya Evelyn, "Alexandria Ocasio-Cortez Thought She 'Was Going to Die' during Capitol Attack," *The Guardian*, January 13, 2021, accessed April 5, 2021.

221 Katie Glueck, "Ocasio-Cortez Says She Is a Sexual Assault Survivor," *New York Times*, February 1, 2021, accessed February 20, 2021.

AOC's future is unclear, as is the road for many who start businesses. Yet, she is most definitely in the Tier of Expansion as she further defines her brand and champions a better future for members of the BIPOC community and women. We salute her for her incredible courage.

GROWING YOUR BUSINESS DESPITE THE ODDS

Growing a business will take courage. By taking the steps to move forward with our goal, we motivate the next person to do the same. Some ways we can do this are to learn how to:

- embrace our intelligence
- stand up to aggressive people
- value the dignity of employees in our workplace
- align our goals with our values
- provide dignity to employees

Women can feel empowered to grow our companies according to terms that work best for us. We can then salute owners who are growing their businesses and celebrate their vulnerability as they go down paths that are new to them.

If we each take these steps, we collectively own our path forward while changing the mindset of those in our wake. As we share our knowledge, or respectfully listen to the courageous souls who are doing it, we create brighter futures for us all.

CHAPTER NINE

Powerful Networks Pave the Way

———

NO NEED FOR WOMEN TO SIT DOWN

"Why don't they sit down?" I vented to my advisor Tom about this minor annoyance which occurred during two recent Fireside Chat conversations I hosted at my business Malama-Doe, where the guests would not sit down. I knew, and I think the guests did as well, that a seat was waiting for them.

Tom retorted, "They showed up to speak. They don't have to do what you want them to do. If they want to stand, they can stand."

Women are judged often enough. Their femininity, emotional expressions, marital status, childcare situation, and more are always questioned, and societal expectations are placed on their success in these areas. In addition, their "success" must measure up to standards about how good of a role model they are for women, how they handle their emotions, and if applicable, their parenting skills.

For those reasons and the emotional burden that lies behind the weight of each scenario, I invite women to be speakers at my workplace for a Fireside Chat. As they share their story of navigating professional barriers and surpassing milestones to an inspired audience of past, present, or future business owners, I hope their leadership motivates the audience to start and grow businesses. In this setting, I liberate them from the gender stereotypes found in existing research on race, emotion, expression, and gender.

Gender research done by Victoria Brescoll demonstrates women who are overtly expressive, especially when taking control, or under-expressive suffer repercussions.[222] Additionally, if they express themselves in a leadership capacity, such as speaking to a group, they do not fare well in a traditional workplace because of their gender. Apparently, the crucial component of a woman's existence in the workplace is how feminine she is perceived. The ideal feminine traits measured and required change based on the audience.

Femininity is a topic that has progressed little since 1974, when United States gender studies researcher and psychologist Sandra Bem conducted groundbreaking research on traits which she categorized under the terms feminine, masculine, and one where both traits scored highly called androgynous. A result of her research was to create the well-known definitions of masculine, feminine, and androgynous traits used in present-day studies, especially on leadership. The definitions were probably never labeled correctly and

---

222 Victoria L. Brescoll, "Leading With Their Hearts? How Gender Stereotypes of Emotion Lead to Biased Evaluations of Female Leaders," *The Leadership Quarterly* Volume 27, Issue 3 (June 2016): 415-425.

are now, nearly fifty years later, incredibly outdated. For example, her research described **femininity** in terms which included "childlike, flatterable, gentle, gullible," as well as "shy, soft-spoken, sympathetic, tender" and **masculinity** as "acts like a leader" and "ambitious, analytical, assertive." Androgyny was found to be the ultimate gender unifier.[223] Researchers have since found leaders use mainly masculine or androgynous traits and few feminine traits.

I pondered the injustice women face by being judged on their femininity and realized Tom was right, I needed to step away from my role in perpetuating institutional sexism. Women are judged enough. By letting the guests remain comfortably standing, the successes of these awesome women could speak for themselves.

FEMININITY, CULTURE, AND MISCEGENATION

A woman should not be blindsided by microaggressions. Research shows society uses social norms to dictate a woman's ability to lead and ability to maintain "self-control." Women, from every ethnic background, have their professional growth stifled and restrained based on their femininity and self-expression. For example, when expressing a concern at work, Asian American and Caucasian American women must do so quietly as these are the feminine expectations to which they must adhere. On the other hand, Arab American women must express a concern without speaking to avoid appearing angry because of underlying

---

223 Jasmine Abrams, "Blurring the Lines of Traditional Gender Roles: Beliefs of African American Women" (master's thesis, Virginia Commonwealth University, 2012), accessed March 24, 2021.

Muslim stereotypes. Both scenarios reveal unacceptable institutional sexism where women are ostracized and find themselves without a supportive network.[224]

These microaggressions of unspoken stereotypes must be confronted while understanding the role of culture, especially in the institution of work. Oxford languages defines culture as "the customs, arts, social institutions, and achievements of a particular nation, people, or other social group."[225] As noted, within a culture, there are social institutions which include the "mechanisms or patterns of social order focused on meeting social needs, such as government, economy, education, family, healthcare, and religion."[226] If inherent problems in the social institutions of a culture are not addressed, a woman will find herself in a no-win situation lacking professional resources, support, and a network.

When first meeting someone, we make assumptions about their race or ethnicity because of the external appearance of their body shape, hair type, and skin pigmentation. One country which looks at skin pigmentation differently than the United States is Brazil. Over half the population of Brazil, or 91 million people, is either black or mixed ethnicity.[227] As Latin America's largest country in size and population, race is based on appearance and self-classified; it is not based on ancestry.

224 Victoria L. Brescoll, "Leading with their hearts? How gender stereotypes of emotion lead to biased evaluations of female leaders," 415-425.
225 *Oxford University Press*, s.v. "Culture," accessed March 29, 2021.
226 Lumen Learning, s.v. "Social Institutions," accessed March 29, 2021.
227 "Afro-Brazilians," Minority Rights, accessed March 24, 2021.

While people from the United States "often perceive people of mixed ancestry as nonwhite, Brazilians understand race in a continuum and consider not only appearance or descent but also social and economic status."

. FRANCES NEGRÓN-MUNTANER, AUTHOR OF "ARE BRAZILIANS LATINOS? WHAT THEIR IDENTITY STRUGGLE TELLS US ABOUT RACE IN AMERICA."[228]

I first traveled to Brazil for work and was amazed at the miscegenation, or interbreeding of people considered to be biracial or multiracial.[229] [230] Years later, I moved to a similar community in terms of it being a global village where miscegenation is also common, in my current village of Shorewood. I was married to a Brazilian and chose this community for the supportive network of culturally mixed families.

228 Frances Negrón-Muntaner, "Are Brazilians Latinos? What Their Identity Struggle Tells Us about Race in America," *The Conversation*, December 20, 2016, accessed March 24, 2021.

229 Steve Bradt, "'One-Drop Rule' Persists," *The Harvard Gazette*, December 6, 2010, accessed March 24, 2021.

230 *Oxford University Press*, s.v. "Miscegenation," accessed March 24, 2021.

After my firstborn child was born, I wondered with which ethnicity she should identify and discussed it with neighbors. We agreed our situations were not easily found in the box of "Latino" or "Hispanic" on the birth certificate registration. Unsurprisingly, 17 percent of the US population stems from "very different ethnic, racial and national backgrounds" who also grapple with the same question.[231] The inflexible and stifling criteria of selecting a box on ethnicity is challenging for people who are of a culturally mixed background. Thankfully, I had a supportive network around me.

ON THE TABLE

Support needs to be found in neighborhoods, at schools, and especially in the workplace where sisterhood among women is complicated. The authors of *Our Separate Ways: Black and White Women and the Struggle for Professional Identity*, Ella L.J.E. Bell and Stella M. Nkomo, explain how white and black women look at their relationships with each other differently because of their experiences with race, gender, and class. They discuss their book on the Women at Work Harvard Business Review podcast episode of "SisterHood is Critical to Racial Justice."[232] [233] As

231 Pew Research Center, "Chapter 3: The Multiracial Identity Gap," in *Multiracial in America: Proud, Diverse and Growing in Numbers*, ed. by Kim Parker, Juliana Menasce Horowitz, Rich Morin and Mark Hugo Lopez (Washington, D.C.: Pew Research Center. 2015), 40-50.

232 Ella L.J.E. Bell and Stella M. Nkomo, *Our Separate Ways: Black and White Women and the Struggle for Professional Identity* (Brighton: *Harvard Business Review* Press, 2003).

233 Amy Bernstein, Sarah Green Carmichael, and Nicole Torres, "Sisterhood Is Critical to Racial Justice," June 8, 2020, in *Women at Work*, produced by Harvard Business Review, podcast, MP3 audio, 1:05:10.

women's network groups form at work, the authors explain the focus is on issues which Caucasian American women care about, that of work-family concerns. Yet, black women are so concerned with racism, and the subsequent micro-aggressions, that they cannot solely focus on the goals of the women's group.

"She wants to deal with work-family issues too, but that experience of oppression is beating her to the ground, oftentimes more so. So, the agendas get to be different."

ELLA BELL SMITH, CO-AUTHOR OF *OUR SEPARATE WAYS: BLACK AND WHITE WOMEN AND THE STRUGGLE FOR PROFESSIONAL IDENTITY*[234]

To offer a supportive network, we need to build one which celebrates women creating structural change. Our top priority must be to learn how to listen to women whose needs are not being addressed. This progress will only happen if we have difficult but honest conversations with female colleagues not typically represented. By conducting effective listening sessions, we can truly confront unwelcome workplaces and offer support to women who are not professionally connected and need personal balance.

---

234 Ibid.

As a business owner, I learned how to host and moderate honest conversations through effective listening sessions when trained for an initiative called On the Table, put on by the Greater Milwaukee Foundation.[235] [236]As a table leader, I had to be well-versed in managing groups through effective listening sessions. The initiative's goal was to bridge the divide on issues that mattered to our community.

I selected the table topic of mentorship for women business owners of different cultural backgrounds, knowing it would lead to challenging issues surfacing which attendees would have to navigate. As my business prepared to host tables, we delved into the key drivers of business ownership and prepared to train attendees on the different types of entrepreneurs: sideprenuer, necessity, flexibility, and opportunity.

When the event took place, the attendees discussed the reasoning behind each type of business owner. After our discussions and through effective listening, we better understood the microaggressions stemming from cultural, race, and network power inherent in many women's situations and why many women must own their own path as a business owner. The importance of building a strong and supportive network for women to thrive in spite of institutional sexism and betrayal was apparent. Women needed to be better connected and balanced, and that could happen through network power.

235 "Home," On the Table, accessed January 31, 2021.
236 "Home," Greater Milwaukee Foundation, accessed January 31, 2021.

HOW NETWORK POWER WORKS

As women build their personal and professional brand, they need to understand the importance of Network Power. It plays a key role in their success as defined by the book *Power: Why Some People Have It and Others Don't*. In it, the author Jeffery Pfeffer details

"Power and influence come not just from the extensiveness of your network and the status of its members, but also from your structural position within that network. Centrality matters. Research shows that centrality within both advice and friendship networks produce as many benefits, including access to information, positive performance rating, and higher pay."

Who is in your network, which positions they hold, and who they know matters.[237] More information can be found on the author page on my business MalamaDoe's website.[238]

A woman who recently relocated or switched industries may have a robust network in her former field, and thus has

237 Jeffrey Pfeffer, *Power Why People Some Have It- and Others Don't* (New York City: Harper Business, 2010), 119.
238 "Book by Sheila Long," MalamaDoe, accessed April 7, 2021.

network density. Yet, with the new situation she finds herself in, she does not have the network centrality to grow professionally as her contacts are not local and may not be "central."

We can say the same for BIPOC women, who may or may not be culturally mixed. Their network may be dense in their communities, but they may not have the centrality to grow their professional network elsewhere. Thus, their network may be stunted if they do not gain the expertise needed.

For this reason, women must build one another up and offer needed resources and support. Here are the stories of two women, Jessica Bell and Sharlen Moore, who channeled their desire for change by building supportive networks. Both women were on a mission to change the world, and they both had networks to do so. I celebrated the sharing of their journey by gathering an audience to hear it, and together we built a community.

TWO SIMILAR WOMEN AND THE IMPACT OF A NETWORK

I invited Jessica and Sharlen to speak at my work in October 2017 and 2018, respectively. Both Jessica and Sharlen live near the Milwaukee neighborhood where they went to high school, both married their high school sweethearts, and both have multiple school age children. Sharlen and Jessica started successful businesses following their passion; Jessica's being that everyone should enjoy wine and its consumption should be easily portable and Sharlen's being that of sustaining grassroots leadership for change with a passion for community justice. Jessica is in the world of business and Sharlen in that of nonprofits. They both have lived in and outside of the United States, with Jessica working in Spain and South America, and with Sharlen born and raised in Jamaica and moving to Milwaukee in the 1980s and working as an adult to become a US citizen.[239] Both have a determined work ethic, a strong religious faith, and are tired of the segregation in Milwaukee and find it at odds with their cultural backgrounds.[240] Both women were immensely qualified and incredibly able to transfix an audience on stage. In both instances, I asked neither to sit down.

JESSICA KEEPS ON PITCHING

I knew Jessica more than I did Sharlen. Jessica was in my network and we had many similarities; we were both from Wisconsin, raised our children speaking a second language, and got business degrees from out-of-state but had returned to raise our children in our home state. Over the years, regardless of where I was at personally or professionally, I always knew that Jessica was another woman pioneering business ownership in my neighborhood. As I watched Jessica grow while developing personally and professionally, I knew I had an invaluable role model.

When Jessica came to speak, she was in pitch mode and had just raised $125,000 for her start-up and over $320,000 in a seed round.[241] She asked me if she should sit down, but I could tell

239 "Women Who Inspire: Sharlen Moore," Member Resources, League of Women Voters of Wisconsin, accessed February 4, 2021.

240 Kevin J. Miyazaki and Mary Louise Schumacher, "Interview with Sharlen Moore," This is Milwaukee, accessed April 10, 2021.

241 Molly Dill, "HaloVino to Introduce New Product," *BizTimes*, May 7, 2018, accessed January 31, 2021.

by her energy that would not serve her well. So, I sat back and listened, and no one minded. Jessica served us wine, and we were enjoying the "magic moment" with her Halo Vino wine glasses in our hands, enthralled as we heard her story.

Jessica Bell is a white woman like myself and moved her career from hosting a TV show named *Wisconsin Foodie* to owning My Wine School as a sommelier.[242] Shortly after we met, she created the Halo Vino shatterproof tumblers, all with the help of Facebook feedback, a Kickstarter campaign, and many more intricacies.[243]

Jessica's Fireside Chat enlightened our audience about how to pivot in our career, how to love selling, and the value of finding brand ambassadors. She was incredibly insightful, and we were all inspired.

Jessica has worked in very male-dominated cultures in New York City as an investment banker and in Spain working in the wine industry. She has made a career out of educating wine lovers as a sommelier.[244] She is a business owner with an established network. Yet, despite having every area of network power covered, she felt more penalized as a women entrepreneur while pitching for capital than working in her previous roles in male-dominated areas. Rest assured, Jessica was undeterred and built her network power and business by joining women's groups and incubators. For women

242 "Home," Wisconsin Foodie, accessed January 31, 2021.

243 "Home," Halo Vino, accessed January 31, 2021.

244 Jeanette Hurt, "Sommelier Develops Plastic Wine Glasses That Double as 'Good' Wine Glasses," *Forbes*, September 30, 2018, accessed April 10, 2021.

to prosper as business owners, we need to eliminate gender-based penalties inherent when pitching for capital.

SHARLEN SHINES ON STAGE

Sharlen was new to my network, so asking her to sit down was awkward for me. I learned of Sharlen when a colleague gave her name to me as a potential speaker. After some initial research, I found out about her incredible background devoting her life to social justice and helping teenagers lead. Also, I was awestruck by Sharlen's background. Her community justice initiative uncovered a volatile climate of incarcerated youth in Wisconsin's youth prisons and escalated it. She contacted local elected officials to put an end to it.[245] [246] The press was constantly covering the story of this injustice and the next steps to rectify it.[247] [248]

That night, I wanted Sharlen to be comfortable telling her story. Also, I wanted to bridge the divide between neighbors so we could learn and support her initiatives to give youth a voice in our city, especially since our community borders Milwaukee. When opening Sharlen's Chat, her vivacious speaking style and superb storytelling were clear.

---

245 Patrick Marley, "Crisis at Lincoln Hills Juvenile Prison Years in Making," *Milwaukee Journal Sentinel,* December 17, 2016, accessed February 5, 2021.

246 Laurel White, "Walker Signs Law Closing Lincoln Hills Youth Prison," *Wisconsin Public Radio,* March 30, 2018, accessed February 5, 2021.

247 Sharlen Moore, "Lincoln Hills Closed. Now What's Needed?," *Urban Milwaukee,* August 28, 2018, accessed February 5, 2021.

248 "Gov. Walker Calls for Closing of Lincoln Hills," *WGTD,* January 4, 2018, accessed February 5, 2021.

Sharlen had made a career out of teaching, public speaking, and leadership. She has taught the youth in Milwaukee how to be great speakers and leaders through a social justice approach, transforming their lives by teaching them to use their leadership gifts and by giving them a voice and an opportunity to make change. With the start-ups she runs, Sharlen gives youth a place where they can be with young adults who care about not only their well-being but also ensuring they are respected. Having trained many African Americans in positions of leadership in Milwaukee, she sees the impact as they make huge strides in our community. Sharlen continues to transform the lives of countless youth with her generosity and kind spirit.

Sharlen Moore is a black woman who arrived in Milwaukee as an immigrant in the 1980s. She worked hard to build her network by playing in her neighborhood and, while working at the YMCA, co-created the Team Achievers Program.[249] Her work there led her to co-found Urban Underground in 2000 and, more recently, Youth Justice Milwaukee.[250] [251]

When Sharlen arrived to speak that night at her Fireside Chat, it was clear she was on a mission to educate us and let us know about the help our neighbors a few miles away from us needed on the upcoming vote legalizing marijuana.[252] Also,

249 Kevin J. Miyazaki and Mary Louise Schumacher, "Interview with Sharlen Moore," *This is Milwaukee,* accessed April 10, 2021.

250 "Impact," Join, Urban Underground, accessed January 31, 2021.

251 YouthJusticeMKE, "Sharlen Celebrates Youth," October 23, 2018, Facebook video, 1:42, accessed March 28, 2021.

252 Don Behm, "Pro Pot: Voters Support All Marijuana Advisory Referendums on Tuesday's Ballots," *Milwaukee Journal Sentinel,* updated on November 7, 2018, accessed January 31, 2021.

one of her protégés, David Crowley, was running to be the next Milwaukee County Executive.[253] Sharlen knew how to deal with our white fragility; it was a way of life for people of color in terms of institutional racism, sexism, and betrayal.[254]

Sharlen wanted to tell the story of youth in the city and how the disappearance of funding for programs like the YMCA's after-school program had left a huge void in the lives of neighborhood teens. As we heard her story, the crowd sat awestruck. She humbled us. Sharlen devotes her life to making the lives of children better and helped to educate us, suburban women, about the lives of BIPOC children a few miles away. She left there with many votes from our neighborhood to pass needed reforms and elect public officials she had trained, which will benefit us all.

Sharlen exemplifies how to build Network Power by leading and growing an incredible network. She was nominated by the League of Women Voters of Wisconsin as the Winning Nominee to the Wisconsin Governor's 19th Amendment Centennial Committee.[255] Her example of how to build a community helps us all, from the recently relocated trailing spouse to the woman who has always lived in her neighborhood, from the new mother who just left her job to the empty nester seeking solace from the loneliness, from the single women to the LGBT+ widow, from the Caucasian American

---

253 Bill Glauber and Alison Durr, "Chris Larson, David Crowley Advance to April 7 Election in Milwaukee County Executive Race," *Milwaukee Journal Sentinel*, updated on February 19, 2020, accessed January 31, 2021.

254 Robin DiAngelo, *White Fragility: Why It's So Hard for White People to Talk About Racism* (Boston: Beacon Press, 2018), 18-19.

255 "Women Who Inspire: Sharlen Moore," Member Resources, League of Women Voters of Wisconsin, accessed February 4, 2021.

to the BIPOC business owner, we all need each other. By helping our neighbor and bridging the divide, we can enrich the lives of our neighbors and ourselves.

FINDING A COMMON VOICE

As women, we need to collectively work together to address these inequities and build our voice so that we can have a seat at the table where decisions are being made. We must take a stand when it is easier to remain silent. Creating a strong community is instrumental in building women's network power. By hosting Jessica and Sharlen, along with thirteen other women business owners at my work as Fireside Chat speakers, I aim to build a network of strong, supportive women. When lining up the speakers, I included people who represented the differences within our city because each of our backgrounds allowed us to create an opportunity stemming from our place of greatness.

Jessica's story educates us on how to build and surround ourselves with a supportive network who will advocate for us when needed. Her example and drive to create a reality from her passion of making wine accessible to all gives us courage. For Jessica to build a business manufacturing a product, a plastic wine tumbler, she needed to raise capital in an environment friendly to women. To support her and all female entrepreneurs, we must have more women represented at the table where decisions about financing are made.

Sharlen's story is one of hope. It tells us how by seeing the potential in those around us, we can devote our life to making it better. Her story exemplifies how one person's actions inspire those around them and, before long, build an army of support. Be it for the unfortunate incarceration of countless youth to receive safe treatment while imprisoned, or for elected officials who advocate for our needs while creating a more just system, each of our actions builds on the next.

For progress to continue, women must bond together while better understanding our differences. By actively listening, we understand how each of us is driven by our own unique experiences and perspectives and how each day, we find new ways to act with courage. The role of institutional betrayal resulting from institutional sexism may or may not have played a part in creating our daily reality. Yet, the researcher who coined these terms, Jennifer Freyd, also realizes the critical role courage plays, which led her to found the Center for Institutional Courage to help shape systemic change.[256]

When reeling from the aftermath of betrayal, what each survivor brings to the table is their courage. In this book, I state objectives and give strategies by presenting real people with real situations. By hearing these stories, I hope you are compelled to also use your strength to create incredible opportunities for yourself. By standing up to the inexplicable judgment of femininity, emotional expression, marital status, childcare situation, and more, I hope you courageously move forward while building a solid community foundation and network from which to spring forward.

---

256 "About Courage," Center for Institutional Courage, accessed March 25, 2021.

CHAPTER TEN

Stop Advising Women to Gain Confidence

———

The current Speaker of the House, Nancy Pelosi, had been a stay-at-home mom when a friend told her to run for office.[257] Now, Nancy tells other women to run for office. She has broken the marble ceiling. By being elected to the US Congress and representing our country as the Speaker of the House, while meeting her principal obligation of defending the Constitution of the United States, she crafts and champions legislation that helps women across the country, such as the Violence Against Women Act.[258] Do you think she lacked confidence because she waited for another woman to encourage her to run?

---

257 Walt Hickey, Mariana Alfaro, Grace Panetta, and Taylor Ardrey, "Nancy Pelosi Was Just Re-Elected as House Speaker — Here's How She Went from San Francisco Housewife to the Most Powerful Woman in Us Politics," *BusinessInsider,* January 3, 2021, accessed January 30, 2021.

258 Nancy Pelosi Speaker of the House, "Pelosi Statement on 26th Anniversary of Violence Against Women Act," Nancy Pelosi Speaker of the House press release, September 13, 2020, on the Nancy Pelosi Speaker of the House website, accessed January 30, 2021.

Let me assure you, everything we as a nation have learned about Speaker Pelosi over her career tells us she likely did not lack confidence. She knew how to make up her own mind; she knew she was talented, and she had a mentor in her father, who had served as a US Congressman.[259] Nancy ran because her friend, Representative Sala Burton, asked her to take her place when diagnosed with late-stage colon cancer that ultimately took her life.[260]

When now-Speaker Pelosi was making her decision, unlike men in that situation, she did not see her gender identified in the seats of the Congress. When she ran for the 100th Congress, there were two women seated in the Senate and twenty-three in the House.[261] Congresswoman Nancy Pelosi may not have felt that she belonged in the House. Yet, having grown up near Washington, DC, in Baltimore where her father was the mayor, she had many mentors in her politically active and connected family. Nancy knew she could get the job done if elected.[262]

Leaders charged with solving gender inequality reason there are fewer women leaders because of women's low confidence which stems from no individual choice, "talent," or mentors. More helpful insight comes from research by Lewis Crewe

259 Biographical Directory of the United States Congress, "Alesandro, Thomas, Jr.," Biography, accessed January 30, 2021.

260 Molly Ball, "How Nancy Pelosi Got to Congress," *Sabato's Crystall Ball UVA Center for Politics* (blog), May 8, 2020, accessed January 30, 2021.

261 Biographical Directory of the United States Congress, "Nancy Pelosi," Biography, accessed January 30, 2021.

262 "History of Women in the U.S. Congress," Rutgers Eagleton Institute of Politics, Center for American Women and Politics, accessed January 30, 2021.

and Annie Wang on the imbalance of gender norms and how institutional factors, among others, signal who is welcome and who is not.[263] McKinsey & Company's Diversity and Inclusion arm uses key markers of Equality, Opening, and Belonging to monitor advancement and needed infrastructure to level the uneven playing field. By monitoring these categories, needed change can be implemented.[264] Remember equality, opening, and belonging while learning about this so-called Confidence Gap.

INSTITUTIONAL SEXISM AND BETRAYAL MEET THE CONFIDENCE GAP

In 2011, Dr. Russ Harris developed a mindfulness technique of approaching internal negativity as a key tool to effectively rethink how one handled "fear and anxiety," which soon became a critique of sound decision-making skills as his book *The Confidence Gap: A Guide to Overcoming Fear and Self-Doubt* went on sale.[265]

Another book followed, written by two world news reporters, claiming women lacked confidence called *The Confidence Code: The Science and Art of Self-Assurance—What Women Should Know.* In it, they found women's self-scrutiny of their realistic capabilities stems from "factors ranging from

263 Lewis Crewe and Annie Wang, "Gender Inequalities in the City of London Advertising Industry," abstract, *Environment and Planning A: Economy and Space* 50, no. 3 (May 2018).

264 McKinsey & Co, *Diversity Wins: How Inclusion Matters* (New York: McKinsey & Company, 2020), 5.

265 Russ Harris and Steven Hayes, *The Confidence Gap: A Guide to Overcoming Fear and Self-Doubt* (Durban: Trumpeter, 2011).

upbringing to biology."[266] [267] Their work blames women's lacking self-confidence as the reason why their professional growth stalls and why there is gender imbalance in the workplace. While this information belittling women workers remains discredited, women get the message they are unwelcome. In her 2018 article "Is the Confidence Gap between Men and Women a Myth?" researcher Laura Guillen provides a detailed explanation of the negative repercussions:

The **Confidence Gap** is "one especially pernicious message has been unchallenged for years: that female workers lack the self-confidence of their male peers and this hurts their chances at success. If they were less hesitant and sold themselves better, this logic goes, success would be theirs."

LAURA GUILLEN, "IS THE CONFIDENCE GAP BETWEEN MEN AND WOMEN A MYTH?"[268]

---

266 Katty Kay and Claire Shipman, *The Confidence Code: The Science and Art of Self-Assurance—What Women Should Know* (New York City: Harper Business, *2018).

267 Katty Kay and Claire Shipman, "The Confidence Gap," *The Atlantic*, May 2014.

268 Laura Guillen, "Is the Confidence Gap between Men and Women a Myth?," *Harvard Business Review*, March 26, 2018, accessed April 4, 2021.

Institutional sexism thrives when all women, half of the population, are told they inherently have no confidence. Women, who continue to grapple with the fallout of additional negative stereotypes as they navigate their professional business growth, find it is stifled further when they face one more justified and undisputed workplace barrier. If a woman continues down a path operating as a success in a man's world, she may eventually face Institutional Betrayal. Laura Guillen explains how:

"Underlying all these messages is the belief that although the deck may be stacked against women as a group, individual women can break through the glass ceiling if they make certain choices: forego the trappings of femininity, learn the rules of the male-dominated working world, and assert themselves accordingly. In this framing, the aforementioned structural barriers are hurdles to be leaped over with proper mental training."

LAURA GUILLEN, "IS THE CONFIDENCE GAP BETWEEN MEN AND WOMEN A MYTH?"[269]

269 Ibid.

Below is an example of how I successfully operated in the male-centric environment where I was making inroads to break through the glass ceiling. I did not exhibit this so-called Confidence Gap, and to this day, I pride myself on being extremely courageous.

HALF-CRAZED COLLEAGUE AT A WORK OUTING

In my twenties, I was about one year into my professional career working in technical sales at my company's headquarters. I had helped one of our regional groups meet a large sales goal and the group I assisted decided a cruise to Mexico was in order. They invited seventy employees in the sales team and partner organizations to attend. I made the invite list! The sales celebration was going to be a long weekend cruise from Los Angeles to a few towns south of the border. The goal was for the organizations to bond on the cruise ship and celebrate our hard work over the past year. As my manager at the corporate headquarters told me about my invitation to the trip, my colleagues were green with envy. Yet, when packing my bags, I knew I had earned the invitation. I had done the work, helped my team achieve the sales quota, and needed to be there to forge relationships.

As I arrived outside the cruise ship, I knew the unspoken corporate rules:

1. Keep alcohol consumption to a minimum.
2. The dress code is always "workplace casual."
3. Keep personal relationships and workplace relationships separate.

4. Keep in mind any colleague might be the next boss.

Everyone invited on this outing ranged from age thirty-five to sixty-five, except for one up-and-coming young finance professional woman, age twenty-eight, and me, age twenty-four. I knew I had to be on my best behavior even though I would be surrounded by salespeople who may have a few too many drinks. But it was a corporate environment, albeit on a cruise ship. I knew everyone would be respectful and was excited to board.

On the ship, I felt a sense of belonging and was welcomed by my colleagues. I know we were all celebrating reaching a common goal together. I realized our group was 90 percent men and 10 percent women, making me one of the few women.

A day later, we stopped off in Ensenada, Mexico, and a few colleagues from my group and I entered a local bar. Even though I spoke fluent Spanish and could have mingled with the locals, I knew I was at work and needed to forge relationships with my coworkers. I felt safe with this group and knew they would have my back as I was a young employee from the corporate headquarters.

We made our way over to the bar where nearly everyone was doing shots. A colleague, Ted, who I had never met before, encouraged me to do a shot and I declined. A few minutes later, Ted approached me and assaulted me, shoving me against a wall. My horrified coworkers pulled this crazy colleague Ted off of me, ensured I was alright, and gave Ted a good talking to. Then, my coworkers stood by me for the rest of the time in the bar, telling me Ted was new to the group, had some mental health problems, and we would steer clear of him. They told me they would talk to Ted's manager about what happened.

As they knew I came from the corporate office, was very young, but most importantly was a woman in a male-centric environment, I really appreciate them walking the path with me that night because I was pretty shaken. After recovering, I realized being the only woman made me a misfit. I was in the middle of Brotopia and had the general sense of feeling at risk, in danger, and "fed up."[270] There was nothing I could do about it but keep myself safe from harm.

When I hear statements like "women lack confidence," I wonder if the men and women making those statements have been put in situations where 90 percent of the people surrounding them are different. I wonder if they know about being a woman who has to fear for her physical safety because she never knows when someone is going to decide to harm her.

Do they know how hard it is to bounce back after these ignorant actions? Do they know how it is to constantly show up and put on a face to let everyone know that you're okay, when you have had experiences that have definitely not been okay?

I did not lack confidence that night; I had a tremendous amount of courage. I made all the right choices. I worked and

---

270 Emily Chang, *Brotopia: Breaking up the Boys' Club of Silicon Valley* (New York: Penguin Audio, 2018), Audible audio ed., 5 hr., 22 min.

was awarded the trip because of my efforts, yet few women mentors were around on that trip. I continued to do my job, made more good choices, and found older male mentors to guide me. Yet, I acknowledge that experience added another level of uncertainty to my interest in moving up the corporate ladder, and not because I lacked confidence.

WOMEN AND MEN IN US CORPORATE LEADERSHIP

Research done in 2009 demonstrates professional women rate their own abilities "significantly higher" than their male colleagues rate themselves. Also, women's coworkers ranked them more positively than they ranked other male colleagues.[271] Research and life experience demonstrate when a claim is made that women lack confidence, it actually refers to women lacking the masculine traits apparent in Executive Presence.

"**Executive presence** relates to authority and trustworthiness, which includes projecting confidence. Specific behaviors include: speaking up in meetings, taking up space physically, projecting one's voice, directness and clarity of speech, asserting oneself and promoting one's own ideas

---

271 Herminia Ibarra and Otilia Obodaru, "Women and the Vision Thing," *Harvard Business Review,* January 2009, accessed March 20, 2021.

or work. We read these behaviors as indicators of confidence, and colleagues often infer a lack of confidence when they are absent. Because many of these 'executive' behaviors show up more in men, we perceive a 'confidence gap.'"

HANNA HART, "THE CONFIDENCE GAP IS A MYTH, BUT A DOUBLE STANDARD DOES EXIST: HOW WOMEN CAN NAVIGATE" [272]

Executive presence explains many of the masculine traits defined in Chapter Nine and leads us to the question addressed in the article "Why Do So Many Incompetent Men Become Leaders?" In his research, the author Tomás Chamorro-Premuzic acknowledges men are "consistently more arrogant, manipulative and risk-prone than women." Yet, he believes there is little incentive to remove anyone exhibiting these traits from leadership roles, as they demonstrate the coveted executive presence, mislabeled as confidence.

To assist effective leaders, Chamorro-Premuzic researched how transformational leaders rolled out effective strategies and found women to be more successful. Women

---

272 Hanna Hart, "The Confidence Gap Is A Myth, But A Double Standard Does Exist: How Women Can Navigate," *Forbes*, March 5, 2019.

demonstrated more sensitive, considerate, and humble personalities than men. Also, they had higher emotional intelligence, "which is a strong driver of modest behaviors."[273]

Ideally, leaders should make a concentrated effort to implement best practices to retain women who suffer from workplace microaggressions, especially since study after study demonstrates when women are direct and speak clearly and assertively, they suffer negative repercussions.[274] One particular study demonstrates how women fear backlash after mentioning their accomplishments.

"Women are expected to be both confident and 'prosocial'—demonstrating care and concern for others—while men can promote themselves without showing care for others and not be perceived negatively. Given this reality, simply advising women to demonstrate more confidence is not just bad advice (as it may well backfire); it effectively and

---

273 Tomás Chamorro-Premuzic, "Why Do So Many Incompetent Men Become Leaders?," *Harvard Business Review*, August 22, 2013, accessed March 20, 2021.

274 Meghan I. H. Lindeman, Amanda M. Durik, and Maura Dooley, "Women and Self-Promotion: A Test of Three Theories," *Psychological Reports* 122, no. 1 (February 2019): 219–30.

unfairly places the burden of correcting the gender imbalance on women."

HANNA HART, "THE CONFIDENCE GAP IS A MYTH, BUT A DOUBLE STANDARD DOES EXIST: HOW WOMEN CAN NAVIGATE" [275]

These extra considerations are a huge burden for women. Thus, we do not rush into rash decisions, and take our time before acting. As we can see, success is defined differently for women than men in the workplace. Below is an example of a woman who led the way to open doors for more women. She had little support when starting out, but she definitely had Executive Presence and was a transformational leader.

ANNE IS TOLD SHE IS NOT GOING TO MAKE IT

Anne Machesky was an early entrant in the newer field of financial planning as described in Chapter Four.

When Anne began her career as a financial advisor in 1980, she was told by a mid-level corporate manager that "she would not make it as a planner." When she asked why, he confidently told her she needed to be thinner and drive a newer car. Anne, knowing herself, her values, and what values really mattered to clients, fiercely defended herself. She

---

275 Hanna Hart, "The Confidence Gap Is A Myth, But A Double Standard Does Exist: How Women Can Navigate," *Forbes*, March 5, 2019.

told this manager he was mistaken as success "has nothing to do with [that], what I want to do to help people."

Nearly two decades later, this same manager tried to recruit Anne to join the firm he was with because she had become wildly successful. Anne reminded him of his hurtful words and "put him in his place." She recounts this story to women when speaking at events how she did not let his words deter her. Anne knew she did not "need to look a certain way or have a certain type of car" to be successful.

After the first incident with the mid-level manager who made such hurtful comments, Anne built her planning practice at a different financial firm. She took risks and small steps alongside "women that literally carved that path through the forest" for all of us. She knows they all "made a difference" so that we women can be this far today. Anne described the 1980s as a time when women "found their foothold." She recalled, "It didn't get easier or better, but the door was opened." She had no mentor, no one to tell her the way forward in the industry. What she had in her early years was a desire to learn.

"I was eager. I was passionate. In my mind, I'm equal to you. So every step you take, whether you say that's my place, or I don't have to look like X, that's building confidence. The more you learn about your field, whatever it is, the more risks you take in business can build confidence."

ANNE MACHESKY, FOUNDER & CEO OF
NWYZE COACHING COMPANY

She thought women started to be able to be themselves in the late 1990s and early 2000s. "They **could do** it their way." As I entered the workforce in the early 1990s, Anne and I reminisced about the changes that took place during those decades. We agree that during that time frame, if you did not find your voice, especially in front of a man, it was over. You had to be passionate and speak up or move out of the field because you could be replaced.

As a speaker at several financial services conferences over the years, including the Twin Cities Women in Insurance and Financial Services (WIFS) local chapter and the National WIFS Conference in 2019, Anne tells the above story in keynote speeches to motivate women in the industry. She directs women:

"Take your place, whatever career, whether black, brown, white, short, tall, whatever. Take your place. Because you're there to learn and succeed. Your brain can work

as well as any male brain. And you should
pursue what you need to pursue."

ANNE MACHESKY, FOUNDER & CEO OF

NWYZE COACHING COMPANY

Anne is a tremendous leader to whom we all owe a debt of
gratitude. Our next woman is another incredible woman
who has also laid the groundwork for us.

JANE FINETTE FINDS THE RIGHT FIT

Jane Finette is a woman who made it to the upper echelons of
the top technology companies in Silicon Valley while working
in male-centric environments. When Jane and I met, I was
quite intimidated. She has had an incredible career in technology, a field I worked in, and has made a tremendous impact in
the field I currently work in, social impact. Jane is the author
of *Unlocked—How Empowered Women Empower Women*.[276]

When we speak, Jane puts me at ease and is completely personable. I feel like we are old friends, all of my fears dissi-
pate. In 2014, Jane started The Coaching Fellowship, whose
mission is to "drive the growth and development of young
women social change leaders around the world."[277] She told
me she is concerned about the lack of confidence in women
as 95 percent of the applications received prioritize it as a top

---

276 Jane Finette, *Unlocked—How Empowered Women Empower
Women* (Potomac: New Degree Press, 2021).

277 "About Us," About, The Coaching Fellowship, accessed January 30, 2021.

concern. I let Jane know that I didn't believe in the Confidence Gap. I believe there is a "misfit" in the job alignment. It turns out that Jane understood this all too well.

Having spent most of her career in technology, Jane reminisces about how she entered the field because she needed a job and found one available in technology. She truly wanted to work in art, in which she holds undergraduate and master's degrees, and even founded an art gallery in Berlin. Yet, her story is one of a woman in tech.

Jane, born and raised in England, was the first person in her family to go to college and graduated happily in 1997. She rose the ranks in technology rapidly, beginning her career at Jungle, a precursor to Amazon, which was in Jane's words, "the UK's first really big internet success story." Five weeks away from becoming a traded company with an initial public offering (IPO), the dot-com bubble burst, reducing her company's flotation value by 95 percent, and three hundred employees were fired the next day.[278]

Jane survived that day and eventually became heavily involved in Mozilla, an internet software community whose pledge is "to ensure the Internet is a global public resource, open and accessible."[279] Jane became Mozilla's head of European marketing and a few years later moved to the San Francisco Bay Area when she was put in charge of retaining 500 million users on Firefox, a web browser developed from

278 Richard Wray, "Ten Years after the Crash, the Dotcom Boom Can Finally Come of Age," *The Guardian*, March 23, 2010, accessed April 11, 2021.
279 "Mozilla Manifesto," About, Mozilla, accessed April 4, 2021.

Mozilla.[280] She called it "the job of her life" where she was in charge of all internal marketing engagements for ninety different language versions.

Jane then participated in a leadership development training session for employees. It was a completely unique experience and helped her discover who she really was. Jane left the company afterward because it was then she finally found her calling. She became an entrepreneur in residence at Astia, "a non-profit organization dedicated to identifying and promoting best-in-class, high-growth ventures led by women."[281] In this role, Jane remembers getting really passionate about coaching others. She wished that in her earlier career she had some leadership coaching, or someone to discuss her values with prior to landing in the field which was not a good match for her values. She decided to do something about it, "to create a program which helped young women leaders in the impact space to get access to leadership development."

She got trained as a coach, went to Coaches Training Institute, and created The Coaching Fellowship. She now has "more than 200 pro bono coaches in thirty countries, and still specifically focused on helping young women, social change makers." Over the past six years, she has put over 1,100 women leaders through the program who live in seventy countries. Jane's business is in the Tier of Growth.

Jane has recently stepped into the executive director role at The Coaching Fellowship and takes her role seriously.[282]

280 "Firefox," TechTarget, accessed April 6, 2021.
281 "Home," Astia, accessed January 30, 2021.
282 "About Us," About, The Coaching Fellowship, accessed January 30, 2021.

She believes she may have "the largest group of women social change makers in the world (with responsibility for over 1,100) young women leaders of social change." As new enrollees are coached and enlightened, Jane sets the strategic direction on what she can do with the "collective impact of this group," how to "accelerate" it, and to whom to "direct" it. As the process of improvement is implemented and the program accelerates, more women are accepted and will graduate from the program.

As we discussed the Confidence Gap, Jane told me she wants all of us, regardless of gender, to work in a field "which serves who we are so we could all stop striving to be something we believe we are supposed to be." Jane explained to me what I have been trying to say when I have to answer to why women run start-ups in the service industry.

"Women very often are driven by relationships. We're drawn to do work which impacts humanity positively; there's a reason why women are drawn to industries like education and healthcare because we're ultimately wired for humanity."

JANE FINETTE, EXECUTIVE DIRECTOR
AT THE COACHING FELLOWSHIP

She is now devoted to helping us all work on our self-image, or "ego," effectively so that we do not have to show up for society as they want us. She acknowledged, "Social media, it's all about comparing."

When statements are made that women are "less than" because they do not fit into a setting that is not made for them to fit into, I disagree that it is about their confidence. They need to be in a place which rewards them for what they bring.

Thanks to the strides that Jane, Anne, and others in their shoes took, women are better represented in the workplace. Nowadays, women continue to be excluded, yet they are confident and know they need to take their place.

TIME'S UP IS GIVING WOMEN A VOICE

Thankfully, women are taking leadership roles by using their voice to tell their stories. With these courageous acts, they open up safe places for conversations for other women to share their stories. These are the diversity changemakers, and the impact of their actions will be felt over the next generations.

One such leader is Jean Grow, who we met in Chapter Seven. As you may recall, a few years after closing up her business in advertising, she pursued her PhD in mass communication and her research always focused on diversity, equity, and inclusion. Jean believed we need to look at the imbalance of gender norms and how institutional factors present not only signal, but also ensure, women and members of the BIPOC community are welcome.[283] Jean's research is one with which I agree strongly. If we implement the legislative arm of change, we can impact businesses, which will transform our daily experiences in society and in businesses. Finally, the correct signals can be sent.

Jean wrote a report focused on the Time's Up initiative entitled "Time's Up/Advertising Meets *Red Books*: Hard Data and Women's Experiences Underscore the Pivotal Nature of 2018." In this report, Jean tells the story of how the Time's Up initiative began.[284] Here is how.

The founder of an independent advertising agency empowered her employee to voice her concern about institutional sexism prevalent in the industry. This employee took action to create a safe space for fourteen additional women executives to heal, collaborate, and formulate their next steps. Together, the team used their freedom in this safe space to transform the advertising industry into one where women can thrive. Their actions ignited change resulting in the Time's Up advertising firestorm.[285]

Thankfully, the momentum they created has not ceased. The Time's Up initiative has expanded its reach beyond speaking up against sexual harassment to the overarching goals

283 Lewis Crewe and Annie Wang, "Gender Inequalities in the City of London Advertising Industry," abstract, *Environment and Planning A: Economy and Space* 50, no. 3 (May 2018).

284 Jean M. Grow and Tao Deng, "Time's Up/Advertising Meets *Red Books*: Hard Data and Women's Experiences Underscore the Pivotal Nature of 2018," *Journal of Current Issues & Research in Advertising* (August 7, 2020): 5.

285 Ibid.

of "insisting everyone is safe at work, disrupting the power status quo, and leveling the playing field." The Time's Up initiative has also moved beyond the adverting industry to those of entrepreneurship, entertainment, health care, tech, and more. The actions of a few will ensure there will be lasting change for many.[286]

We need women to work and thrive without facing repercussions because of their gender. Women must bear the weight of sexism alongside their ascent in companies. They need support from not only their workplaces in the above areas, but also from their government. In the United States we lag behind other countries with our laws about gender equality and, consequently, women find themselves working in a truly backward system by receiving unequal pay and treatment. Let's hear how other countries, in cooperation with the United Nations, work toward achieving gender parity.

THE UNITED NATIONS' ROLE IN ERADICATING DISCRIMINATION AGAINST WOMEN

The United States does not give women the same rights in the US Constitution. In "eighty-five percent of U.N. member states, their constitutions explicitly guarantee equality for women and girls." Yet the United States falls short because of the failure to pass the Equal Rights Amendment which Phyllis Schlafly's crusade diligently opposed.

---

286 "Our Work," Times Up Now, accessed January 30, 2021.

"The Convention on the Elimination of All Forms of Discrimination against Women, or CEDAW, is an international legal instrument that requires countries to eliminate discrimination against women in all areas and promotes women's equal rights. CEDAW is often described as the international bill of rights for women. The United Nations adopted CEDAW on 18 December 1979. As of 2016, 189 countries have ratified CEDAW."[287]

As of December 2020, 114 member states ratified the *Optional Protocol to the Convention on the Elimination of All Forms of Discrimination against Women (OP-CEDAW)*. A key benefit is the independent process to address human rights violations.

"(The OP-CEDAW offers) remedies for the individual victim such as compensation and reparation, as well as more general recommendations for structural or systemic changes the State party concerned should implement to prevent reccurence of the violation (enactment of legislation, training of lawyers and law enforcement officials,

---

287 Pooja Khanna and Zachary Kimmel with Ravi Karkara, *Convention on the Elimination of All Forms of Discrimination Against Women (CEDAW) for Youth* (New York: United Nations Entity for Gender Equality and the Empowerment of Women, 2016).

ensuring access to justice, awareness raising programmes, etc.)."

UNITED NATIONS HUMAN RIGHTS OFFICE

OF THE HIGH COMMISSIONER[288]

Many violations are reviewed and fixed with changes made in each country with the impetus of having the CEDAW ratified. For example, in 2015, violations from Canada of "high levels of violence faced by aboriginal and indigenous women, including disappearances and murders" and in 2018 in Kyrgyzstan with "bride kidnapping" were addressed by setting key precedents and not blaming the victims for a lack of executive presence.

Algeria, a service-oriented culture in an Islamist nation in Northern Africa, has benefited from ratifying CEDAW. Equal pay and treatment are a non-issue because of their legal system's understanding of the need for gender equality. Additionally, Algeria provides free education. When girls do well in math or science in high school, they normally go directly to college to study science or medicine; the number of doctors is "almost at parity" in terms of gender, and scientists are primarily women. The high number of Algerian women who are lawyers and judges ensures a women's perspective is

---

288 UN Office of the High Commissioner for Human Rights (OHCHR), "20 years from the entry into force of the Optional Protocol to the Convention on the Elimination of All Forms of Discrimination against Women (OP-CEDAW): A universal instrument for upholding the rights of women and girls and for their effective access to justice," *United Nations Human Rights Council News,* December 10, 2020, accessed April 11, 2021.

represented when laws are made. Because of this structure in place, many women own pharmacies or run family-owned businesses, and their professional opinions are valued.[289]

Yet, in the United States, with the proliferation of the gender imbalance and unequal pay, we blame women for their lack of executive presence and confidence gap. It is time the United States government and its citizens owned our backwardness and lack of progress by seeing what has been clearly demonstrated through the many good examples of what is possible. We have zero excuses as a country. This picture of equality is not a pipe dream; it is absolutely possible.

WHAT WE CAN DO

Advising women to gain confidence is counterproductive. Women working in outdated companies needed to walk the path of proving they could operate in a man's world by using the executive functions of speaking up, taking up more physical space, and projecting and articulating their voice.[290] However, women were, and are, justified in feeling insecure about their futures.

Thankfully, there has been ratification by thirty-eight of the states in the United States for an Equal Right Amendment (ERA) to be added to the US Constitution.[291] To make your voice known, follow the Feminist Majority online.

---

289 Meriem Boudjadja, Interview with author, August 21, 2020.
290 Hanna Hart, "The Confidence Gap Is A Myth, But A Double Standard Does Exist: How Women Can Navigate," *Forbes*, March 5, 2019.
291 "The United States Must Guarantee Equality on the Basis of Sex in the Constitution," *Equality Now* (blog), July 2, 2020, accessed on February 1, 2021.

"It's time for supporters everywhere to write, call, text, email and meet with their Senators. 2021 can be the year that women are included in the Constitution with the ERA as the 28th Amendment and the year that VAWA (Violence Against Women Act) is again reauthorized in the law."

ELEANOR SMEAL, PRESIDENT, FEMINIST MAJORITY[292]

By passing the ERA, we will see women empowered to exit unsafe or unfair working conditions when companies are held accountable for reparations. With this safety net, women can start from an even playing field, reenter work-forces, and receive equal pay, a win-win for all. As companies create ideal safe, secure, and fair cultures that are fully inclusive of women, everyone benefits with all employees receiving equal pay, being heard, and thriving.

One consulting firm which systematically categorizes change in Diversity and Inclusion in a thorough and consistent man-ner is McKinsey & Company. By setting goals based on their

292 "Statement by Eleanor Smeal, President, On the Equal Rights Amend-ment and the Violence Against Women Act," Feminist Majority press release, March 17, 2021, on the Feminist Majority website, accessed March 22, 2021.

objectives of Equality, Opening, and Belonging, they capture what needs to addressed, monitor its advancement, and incorporate needed infrastructure changes.[293]

- By addressing equality, women can use their own feminine qualities to create more voice and agency as they work and thrive without facing repercussions because of their gender.
- By creating an environment of openness, women will have a stronger impact in the workplace as we create a world where women can show up and be fully present.
- By measuring belonging, women will garner enough respect so equality and progress can happen.

Let's transform the landscape for women. By creating safe spaces to educate women, we can create massive change. By using the power of problem solving and collaboration in group settings, women have the potential to create massive impact. One such example is the Time's Up initiative, which is a direct response to the need for change. More information on how can be found on my author page at my business MalamaDoe's website.[294]

---

293 McKinsey & Co, *Diversity Wins: How Inclusion Matters* (New York: McKinsey & Company, 2020), 5.

294 "Book by Sheila Long," MalamaDoe, accessed April 7, 2021.

CHAPTER ELEVEN

Entrepreneurs Who Inspire Us

GROWTH AND SUCCESS DEFINED DIFFERENTLY

"What do you mean they are unsuccessful?" I sat incredulously looking at my trusty advisor, Thomas P. Leisle Jr., as we discussed the tiers of the Awesome Women Incubator Model. I had just explained how in the first two Tiers of **Discovery** and **Canvasser,** a woman is laying the groundwork for her company. Then, as she builds her business, she heals, thrives, and celebrates her strengths as she evolves into the Tiers of **Growth, Prosperer, Fulfillment,** and **Expansion.** Tom had just told me the only successful businesses were the ones in the Tier of Expansion or those rapidly approaching it.

"I think the other businesses should be much further along than they are," Tom responded. "The ones in the Tiers of Growth, Prosperer, and Expansion serve a niche and exceed revenue year after year, but they need to do it faster. I am not alone in my thinking; other people agree with me."

Tom was talking about the Opportunity Entrepreneurs as being "successful" businesses. I agreed with him from a dollars-and-cents point of view and based on everything written in financial publications or about coveted speakers. In the Tier of **Expansion**, women are comfortable with debt and seek to grow, develop professionally, and polish their motivational speaking expertise. He felt as most men of his age and ethnic background did—white men over the age of fifty.

Women who arrive in the Tier of **Growth** become Opportunity Entrepreneurs. They have a "strong personality" defined as a "general strength of character" by the blog *A Conscious Rethink*.[295] When these women, and others, honestly and courageously voice their personal and professional stories, they liberate other women to follow suit. In turn, a plethora of powerful and assertive women authentically engage in support of one another.

Although I respected Tom, I disagreed with him on the above point. In my world, very few women I meet outside of my professional life run their own business. The ones who I meet end up working in the first Tiers of **Discovery, Canvasser,** and **Growth** as a Flexibility Entrepreneur so they can care for their children and work on the side. They need to work yet have additional responsibilities which they can balance by being a business owner.

In my case, hands down, the most successful entrepreneurs are the Flexibility and Necessity Entrepreneurs. They launch

---

295 "13 Signs You Have A Strong Personality That Might Scare Some People," *A Conscious Rethink* (blog), updated on August 22, 2019, accessed March 17, 2021.

a business and keep it going despite tremendous odds. The caveat was that of the women Opportunity Entrepreneurs I met; they started out as the Flexibility and Necessity Entrepreneurs that were being shunned in my conversation with Tom. I knew that by helping the women needing support in the beginning Tiers of the model of **Discovery, Canvasser,** and **Growth,** we fill the pipeline for a larger group of women to arrive in the Tier of **Expansion.**

As Tom and I parted ways in a room filled with tension, I updated my model to reflect how success is defined by women, which serves as a gate for a woman to exit one tier and enter the next. Success is defined as the following, for a woman leaving the Tier of:

- **Discovery** setting up a bank account and legal entity
- **Canvasser** getting paying customers
- **Growth** hiring staff
- **Prosperer** contributing financially to pet causes and society
- **Fulfillment** fine-tuning their skills as an accomplished speaker
- **Expansion** repeating the tiers all over again with another business

No matter how far women succeed, two topics of conversation will be heard incessantly: Why don't women's businesses grow? Why don't they hire employees?

WHY DON'T WOMEN RUN HIGH-GROWTH BUSINESSES?

What the questioners seek to understand must be clarified. Are they referring to high-growth companies? Normally they are, and they fail to realize that male and female "firms that become high growth" only include 2 percent of total businesses, which are defined as experiencing

---

"more than 70 percent employment growth over a three-year period are (firms) ten years or older. At the same time, high-growth firms tend to be small - 76 percent of them have fewer than twenty employees at the outset of the (three-year) high-growth period."

GOLDMAN SACHS VOICE OF SMALL BUSINESS
IN AMERICA 2019 INSIGHTS REPORT[296]

Few businesses qualify as high growth, especially not start-ups. The question about hiring employees is more complex.

Only in the Tier of **Expansion**, founders hire more than six employees. Since 1972, the rate women opened businesses

---

296 Goldman Sachs, *Voice of Small Business in America: 2019 Insights Report* (New York: Goldman Sachs, 2019), 6.

grew eight times, having increased from 4.6 percent to 42 percent in 2019. Yet, they only grew the workforce 8 percent and increased revenues 4.3 percent.[297] The answer of why lies in the Tier of Growth, and while women are starting businesses, we aren't hiring employees, with raw 2012 US Census data showing 89.5 percent of women-owned businesses employ only the business owner. Research shows that as women business owners' experience and business acumen grow, their rate of entrepreneurial activity actually increases at a much slower pace than male counterparts.[298]

Here is an inspirational story about a woman who grew a business and bypassed the Tier of Fulfillment to arrive at the Tier of Expansion.

HANNAH ANDERSON AND THREEPAWS GOURMET

Hannah Anderson is the founder and owner of Threepaws Gourmet, an organic, plant-based dog treat company who was what Tom would characterize as "successful." She operates in a niche market where she has a strong background and supportive family.

Hannah's journey began, rescue pup by her side, in her home kitchen. She explained, "The idea was to pull inspiration from fun boutique store bakery biscuits that weren't readily

297 American Express, *The 2019 State of Women-Owned Business Report* (New York: American Express, 2019), 3.

298 Dolores Rowen, *Veteran Women & Business: A Data Resource: Employing the U.S. Census Survey of Business Owners and Self-Employed Persons and the Annual Survey of Entrepreneurs to Develop a Profile of Veteran Women-Owned Firms* (Washington DC: National Women's Business Council, 2017), 5.

available, give them a healthy superfood makeover, and offer them to the masses." When Hannah's business outgrew her home in Whitefish Bay, Wisconsin, she partnered with the Eisenhower Center, a Milwaukee gem, to make her treats with the same love, passion, and compassion she did. The Center has a great purpose: to provide vocational training and jobs for adults with disabilities, which to Hannah is important, saying, "It's not just a job, it's a supportive and transformative atmosphere to learn, grow, and build confidence."

Sustainable business growth has always been important to Hannah. One of the most exciting milestones was when she felt Threepaws Gourmet could support her enough to leave her full-time job. She remembers, "It was definitely a leap of faith. But thankfully, each passing year continues to add validation to that decision. I left my job for maternity leave and never returned." Today, Hannah has two small children aged two and four that keep her busy, but not once has she ever considered giving up on growing her business. A compelling example was when she won first place in "The Dolphin Pool," a local shark-tank-style competition. She recalled, "I remember feeding my five-week-old baby before and after presenting—it was crazy!"

Hannah's determination paid off. This year, 2021, is quickly becoming her biggest year yet with a full product launch on Chewy, a national distributor. She had support along the way: "My husband Sam has been an amazing help from day one and I'm a huge believer in how no one gets anywhere alone. I have many people to thank for where I am today. If you have an idea that keeps coming back, listen to it. A good idea doesn't come and go, it comes and grows."

Hannah's story is a great one, telling us about women who had support. Some women walk down a different path. Here are inspirational stories of women who not only took on employees but took on debt to grow their business to arrive in the Tier of Expansion.

CLEISE BRAZILIAN DAY SPA

Cleise Gomes came to the United States from Brazil where she had three children, all high school graduates, with her common-law husband. After their twenty-year relationship ended, she arrived in Chicago in search of a new beginning at age thirty-nine with only five hundred dollars to her name. She had one friend, her husband's coworker, who picked her up at the Chicago airport and set her up as his sixty-year-old Brazilian nanny's roommate. Alone and afraid, she feared she would not reach her full potential in a new country.

Cleise left a career with decades of work experience as an aesthetician, or skin care specialist, in Brazil. She worked with nutritionists, plastic surgeons specializing in dermatology, and knew a lot about skin. In her new home of Chicago, Cleise faced the expected microaggressions as she was a non-English speaker and immigrant, yet she was motivated to learn English and wanted to make money and build her career.

She worked as an aesthetician for different spas for years as a Necessity Entrepreneur. Then, she recalls, "My clients told me, 'You offer something unique.' I started thinking about owning a business." Since her funds were limited, she let tips accumulate in an unopened box.

When she was ready to open her business, she found she had accumulated over ten thousand dollars in tips and many business cards. By exchanging her clientele's expertise for her complimentary spa services, Cleise received needed help with bank laws, her lack of credit history, and zoning. She then set up shop in the upscale Chicago neighborhood of Lincoln Park for five years. Later, with her daughter as an investor, she moved and purchased a building with a parking lot in the nearby trendy River West. She has been there for ten years.

Cleise is now the proud owner of Cleise Brazilian Day Spa in downtown Chicago.[299] Her spa plays Bossa Nova music and employs ten aestheticians who she interviewed and hired. She set up a process where they sign a contract, enter personalized training, then read and follow her protocol. She offers Brazilian wax, Bossa Nova Facials, and a unique skin routine for acne treatment, among other services. When her clients tell her they don't feel like they are in Chicago, she explains, "My music is friendships."

What I love about what Cleise did is she took out a loan to expand her business to strategically grow, instead of using it for what most business owners require financing for, "to improve cash flow, manage working capital, and maintain operations."[300] Should more people do what she did? Funding a business is another emotionally charged subject for both men and women.

299 "Welcome," Cleise Brazilian Day Spa, accessed February 21, 2021.
300 Goldman Sachs, *Voice of Small Business in America: 2019 Insights Report* (New York: Goldman Sachs, 2019), 5.

FUNDING & SERVICE OFFERING

Businesses require funding, and our feelings about funding invariably impact our ability to grow. Yet to make money to pay off the funding, we must sell a service or product. However, even if we are a product-based company, the services we offer matter. We must provide a service offering that brings value to a customer. At each of the tiers, business owners experience different feelings about funding. Here is the breakdown for a woman in the Tier of:

- **Discovery** is guilt-ridden while aiming to be a business owner
- **Canvassing** is guilt-ridden while creating her service offering
- **Growth** develops her business offering while streamlining her services
- **Prosperer** is comfortable with debt while actively selling her services
- **Fulfillment** is unconcerned and earns profits while contributing to pet causes
- **Expansion** is interested in additional debt to expand and refine her offering

Wendy K. Baumann, the president/CVO of The Wisconsin Women's Business Initiative Corporation (WWBIC), leads a nonprofit devoted to offering resources to women entrepreneurs, including business and financial training as well as direct lending to secure financing. I'm one of the many women who benefited from her contributions. She has moved WWBIC well into the Tier of Expansion by redefining her service offering continuously.[301]

---

301 "About WWBIC," WWBIC, accessed February 21, 2021.

WENDY K. BAUMANN JOINS WWBIC

The Wisconsin Women's Business Initiative Corporation (WWBIC) was an idea that began in the halls of the YWCA of Greater Milwaukee.[302] In 1987, the CEO and president of the YWCA of Greater Milwaukee, Julia Taylor, was migrating from the "Swim & Gym" model to stay in line with the greater YWCA initiative focused on the women's movement. Together with her board, she was actively involved in meeting the needs for women, especially minorities and low-wealth individuals, through women's entrepreneurship. One solution that arose was a new and innovative idea, which needed support to launch, of creating what is now WWBIC.

Julia and the YWCA board formulated the plan to move the idea into a formidable project. With the board's extreme commitment to the idea's evolution, they secured funding, resources, and leadership to bring basic education, training, and financing to women. Thanks to their efforts, the idea of WWBIC was realized and, after a few years, became a separate nonprofit with support from the YWCA.

In 1994, Wendy had been working at the Milwaukee Area Technical College (MATC) as the director of small business development.[303] In this role, she housed small business incubators focusing on helping primarily minority and lower-income individuals and was contemplating a long-term career at MATC. She recalls, "I really liked my job."

---

302 "Home," YWCA Southeast Wisconsin, accessed February 21, 2021.
303 "Home," Milwaukee Area Technical College, accessed February 21, 2021.

Wendy previously was the executive director of The Hispanic Chamber of Commerce of Wisconsin.[304] She had strategically modified its structure, resulting in state and national recognition, increased membership by over 500 percent, and the receipt of the "Hispanic Chamber of the Year" honor from the US Hispanic Chamber of Commerce.[305]

After WWBIC's last executive director exited, Wendy was referred by a colleague and casually applied. When she was offered the role in 1994, she knew it was a challenging position which required solid leadership. However, Wendy was not one to be overcome by obstacles. She recognized WWBIC served women whose professional growth had been stifled and were isolated without resources and support. Wendy knew WWBIC had sound business education and, as their leader, she could help women reach their full potential as business owners, even in the face of institutional sexism. She accepted the role, not quite knowing what was in store for her.

The CEO who hired her, Julia Taylor, sat on WWBIC's board for years afterward and acknowledges, "Wendy is a life force who made the agency what it is. She developed a story board and made WWBIC a major intermediary where she could bring lending dollars to the table." Julia is amazed to see how it has grown and all that has become possible twenty-seven years later.

---

304 "Home," United States Hispanic Chamber of Commerce, accessed March 17, 2021.

305 Ibid.

Wendy devoted her career to creating an equitable workplace for women. She helped thousands of women transform themselves into business owners. Wendy did this by navigating through dialogue and successful collaboration with public, private, and diverse groups, leading to WWBIC's incredible growth.

Her efforts have not gone unnoticed. Wendy has sat on over fifteen local and national boards and currently is a member of at least fifteen more, which she describes as a key driver in her success. She has received over twenty local, statewide, and national awards, including multiple recognitions from the Small Business Administration.[306] She has spearheaded five major initiatives transforming the Milwaukee region. One such initiative was microlending to main street communities through Kiva.

KIVA AND WWBIC

WWBIC helps women business owners with inadequate funding grow professionally with autonomous access to flexible and convenient financial tools through Kiva, which offers zero-percent-interest loans to women through crowdfunding.[307] Wendy K. Baumann ensured both WWBIC and Kiva would service women business owners statewide. Because of Wendy's efforts and success in bringing Kiva loans to Wisconsin, she gave my business an opportunity to grow. With a Kiva loan, it gave me the professional and financial support to hire interns and grow my business by

---

306 "Home," Small Business Administration, accessed March 17, 2021.
307 "Home," Kiva, accessed February 21, 2021.

participating in a Kiva microlending initiative through WWBIC. I was not alone.

As of February 2021, Kiva Wisconsin has fulfilled 363 loans, bringing crowdfunding for this platform to $2,223,900. It has serviced an average loan size of over $6,100. These loans serve mainly women who need autonomous access to capital, with 68 percent reporting being female, and 55 percent being people of color who oftentimes face microaggressions stemming from institutional sexism and betrayal.[308]

Throughout COVID-19, WWBIC has put 85 percent of its business and financial training online and on demand. Wendy recalls, "I have never worked so hard in my life, and I was a hard worker before." Her staff has learned DocuSign and how to close loans virtually. When thinking of her staff, Wendy acknowledges her immense pride in their work.

WWBIC has been a true testament to assisting women. Their website reads, "WWBIC has provided quality business and financial education coupled with access to fair capital and financial products since 1987. WWBIC's impact is seen through the many entrepreneurs, business owners and individuals whom we assist."[309]

CIRCLE OF INFLUENCE
The value Wendy created growing WWBIC, and Cleise by opening her spa, is to proactively impact an area where a lack

---

308 Michelle Sherbinow, e-mail message to author, February 22, 2021.
309 "Home," WWBIC, accessed February 21, 2021.

of access to professional networks could have stifled many women's professional business growth. By not acquiescing or tolerating institutional sexism, they owned their own path as business owners and subsequently grew their sphere of influence. They did the number-one habit which Dr. Steven Covey recommends in his book, *The 7 Habits of Highly Effective People*: own the outcome by making a difference in their world.[310] There are two ways to look at choice as described below, and with a growth mindset we own our future.

"The Freedom to choose. Instead of reacting to, or worrying about, conditions over which they have little or no control, proactive people focus their time and energy on things they can control. The problems, challenges, and opportunities we face fall into two areas—Circle of Concern and Circle of Influence."

"HABIT ONE: BE PROACTIVE" *THE 7 HABITS OF HIGHLY EFFECTIVE PEOPLE*[311]

---

310 Steven R. Covey, *The 7 Habits of Highly Effective People: Powerful Lesson in Personal Change* (New York: Free Press, 2004).

311 Franklin Covey, "Habit 1: Be Proactive," The 7 Habits of Highly Effective People, accessed February 18, 2021.

By focusing on our Circle of Influence, we make an impact. Our actions are seen and felt by ourself, our friends, our colleagues, and our acquaintances. The people who we let into our life impact our current and future success.[312] [313] One person who I let into my life, Amanda Baltz, who we met earlier in the book, continues to grow professionally and reach her full potential.

AMANDA BALTZ ON GROWTH

Amanda Baltz runs a health care start-up that is an innovative health care cardiac partner. She took some major steps to grow her business. While pregnant with her fifth child, Amanda traveled to Brazil and Mexico City and showcased a new "hand-held, electrocardiograph device to provide a heart reading on smart devices in seconds."[314] Her goal was to facilitate home health care. She wanted to see the potential for its use with patients who did not have autonomous access to flexible and convenient tools, yet truly needed the high-quality medical care Amanda's product and company could provide.

She witnessed how this product will save the lives of the most vulnerable, who were isolated and afraid, lacking resources and support. She tells me when witnessing her product working on the trip, "I literally got weak in the knees and started crying. I realized that all this work we had been tolling away, heads down, in little West Bend, Wisconsin, is in the heart

312 Blaze Kos, "Relationship Circles – the Most Important Diagram of Your Life," *Relationships* (blog), AgileLeanLife, accessed February 18, 2021.

313 Blaze Kos, "Healthy Relationships Are What Matters Most in Life," *Relationships* (blog), AgileLeanLife, accessed February 18, 2021.

314 "Take ECGs In-Home," Spaulding Medical, accessed February 21, 2021.

of some of these really vulnerable populations, doing really good things. That was God's way of telling me, like, you had a job to do here, so you better show up."

Amanda returned home from that trip, wrote the business plan, and spun off this product and service from the parent company. Her goal was to offer equitable health care. She created a new company called Spaulding Medical, which provides "cardiac insights for transformative patient care and research."[315]

When creating Spaulding Medical, Amanda became more fiscally conservative than her parent organization, Spaulding Clinical. That is, until recently, when a top-ten health care system contacted them to be an innovative cardiac partner, which converted Spaulding Medical into an innovation company overnight. She calls it a "thrilling and scary ride of an entrepreneur where (she) has to maintain partnerships, find the investments, manage an operational team, and maintain culture and morale."

As this was not enough, this all happened during a pandemic with her five children having to be educated in their home. This was quite a challenge, yet Amanda remembered:

"That moment in Brazil, that moment in Mexico, and the mission of what we're doing, I realize I have to keep showing

---

315 "Home," Spaulding Medical, accessed February 21, 2021.

up for it. When you work in health care technology and you see that the technology can save lives, you go. You know it's worth it to step out of your safe little world of black and make yourself uncomfortable and go get the job done. It's gonna be really hard but go and get it done. That's the world that I live in now."

AMANDA BALTZ, CO-FOUNDER & CEO
OF SPAULDING MEDICAL

Today, the Spaulding 12-lead ECG product line is in use in over thirty-five countries.[316]

DOYENNE ON PASSING THE TORCH

Prior to launching my business, I was thrilled to find a like-minded group of women two hours away in Madison. The group, called The Doyenne Group, focuses on strengthening "entrepreneurial ecosystems that invest in the power and potential of women entrepreneurs."[317] Over the past few years, they have worked with many women entrepreneurs, including myself, with an inspiring energy.

---

316 "Take ECGs In-Home," Spaulding Medical, accessed February 21, 2021.
317 "Our Mission," About Us, Doyenne Group, accessed February 21, 2021.

I met their founders in November 2016 and, in them, I found a truly supportive network for entrepreneurs who are women. They launched their business a few years ahead of me, in 2012, to help unify women feeling isolated and give them access to tools and a professional network. They realized women are blindsided by microaggressions because of institutional sexism and betrayal.

Their co-founder, Amy Gannon, sat with me often to encourage the growth of my company as I moved from the Tier of Discovery to Prospering. She epitomized women truly passing on a lit torch from one to the next in the spirit of helping one other. Tragically, Amy and her daughter perished in a helicopter crash in late 2019 while on vacation.

While mourning the loss of her co-founder, Heather Wentler has continued on as executive director and has continued to lead the organization into a pivot to virtual programming available to entrepreneurs around the country. Heather served on my business's advisory council in 2019, and I am blessed to call her a friend. From working with both Amy and Heather, I am a testament to how the light from the torch they pass still burns. They were founded "to right two wrongs. First, to eliminate the gender gap in the entrepreneurial community and second, because they were tired of asking repeatedly, 'Where are all the women?'"

As the Doyenne Group fine-tuned the service offering in the home market of Madison, in 2018 they rolled out their streamlined services to Milwaukee. Over the next few years, they will continue to grow their influence as they expand to new cities as a solid partner to women entrepreneurs. I look forward to seeing the impact of their future growth.

SUPPORT AND RESOURCES NEEDED

Each one of these women shaped my future. I met some personally and others professionally, and each one paved the path to make it easier for women, of which I was a benefactor. The courage of each of these women inspired me to act.

In this book, we witness how women:

- leave their careers because they
  - lack balance, support, and fulfillment and must start over professionally (Chapter One)
  - realize insurmountable ceilings are in place in institutions where they work and face institutional betrayal (Chapter Five)
  - lack executive presence and must correct the gender imbalance (Chapter Ten)
- launch a business and
  - discover life and professional balance with a supportive work culture (Chapter Four)
  - fill out the canvas to experience a sense of belonging (Chapter Six).
- grow a business and
  - adapt their lifestyle as they become Opportunity Entrepreneurs (Chapter Three)
  - confront sexism as they prosper (Chapter Seven)
  - grow while blindsided by microaggressions because of institutional sexism (Chapter Eight)

- face demanding femininity, race, and network stereotypes (Chapter Nine)
- venture down uncharted waters and inspire us (Chapter Eleven).

For more women to grow businesses, we need to support them. As women's businesses grow and owners courageously use their voice in the face of resistance and microaggressions, let's use our common voice to stand in solidarity and support of them. To stop history from repeating itself for women and perpetuating a dismal future for women into the next generations, let's help women navigate professional barriers. We must interrupt the institutional sexism and betrayal that inhibits women who are:

- exiting promising successful accomplished careers
- feeling shunned when they arrive in a new market
- finding themselves professionally disconnected
- experiencing their own diminishing personal and professional brand because they are not thriving professionally

In doing so, we stop repeating the problems of the past and leaving the same dire legacy for our children and grandchildren. Let's recognize the inequity of resources and support and be prepared to respond accordingly when we witness it. In doing so, we offer our support for women daily and they will feel our compassion and appreciate the privacy and space we give them.

Let's celebrate alongside women, champion their needs, and recognize their strength as we applaud them for having the courage to advocate for themselves as they find the needed balance. Women need resources and support. We can help by taking a small step of voicing our support for the Time's Up movement on social media, or the larger step of contacting our elected officials to ratify the US Constitution and add the Equal Rights Amendment. Also, we can make a large impact in our day-to-day lives.

My goal of this book is for women to become safe, happy, healthy, and strong connected professionals. By forging a common partnership with women, we create an equitable workplace for women. We see women growing and thriving through their personal and professional brands, glad to have had the opportunity to transform themselves.

Thank you for taking the time to listen to the stories of the women in this book. Please share them as another small step in inspiring others to welcome, encourage, and respect women. Together, we can create a world where we lead by example and motivate more awesome women to be a part of a new model for success in business and entrepreneurship for the next decade.

Let's expand and grow.

PART FOUR

TIPS AND TOOLS

Stories from Women Who Inspired Me

FOCUS ON THE FUTURE AND FORGET UNREALIZED PLANS

Impatiently, Mary Ellen explained to her children, "Tomorrow is another day. Let's get started." She had lived an eventful life and was always ready for the next adventure.

Mary Ellen Long was my grandmother, born in 1912 in my hometown of Grand Chute, Wisconsin, where she resided her entire life. Raised on a horse farm, she knew farming, agriculture, and cooking. Yet, she was proudest of her education, having been a member of her high school's first graduating class.

Upon graduation, Mary Ellen's father planned to have her fulfill her dream of opening a hat store in downtown Appleton, the neighboring big city. To gain some business sense, she attended the local liberal arts college, Lawrence University. The year was 1932, and twenty-year-old Mary Ellen was a woman breaking down barriers.

My grandmother never did open that hat store. She broke down barriers, but not the ones she initially intended. That very same year, tragedy struck the family when her father climbed their front yard tree to trim it, and unfortunately fell, broke his neck, and died. The entire family was shaken, most of all her mother who was saddened and did not cope well. Mary Ellen, being the oldest child, took over responsibility for the family. She dropped out of Lawrence University, and as the family needed money, took a job at Kreskies, Appleton's downtown convenience store.

She also took care of her seven younger siblings, aged seven to nineteen. As her mother did not adjust well to life as a widow, Mary Ellen regularly drove her to the cemetery to visit her father's grave and learned a hard lesson. She would not end up lacking independence. At age twenty, Mary Ellen took action and focused on the future.

Five years later, Mary Ellen married my grandfather Walter, or Wally. Shortly thereafter, they purchased a farm with cows that needed to be milked. Mary Ellen managed workers who handled the cows. Over the next nine years, she bore five children. As she cared for them, she simultaneously helped her three youngest siblings with their farms, daily lives, or childcare. Mary Ellen cooked and fed the children, workers, and relatives daily with three hearty meals. She was a hard worker who was emotionally and physically drained, yet she was not a complainer.

As time went on, Mary Ellen and Wally purchased a second farm which required her hiring and managing more workers, some of whom were key right-hand men. Mary Ellen managed the farms entirely on her own with their help. She was tired from the constant work but made her home a gathering place for local neighbors, farmers, and family who would stop in looking to share friendship and local news which she knew from her husband, Wally, who was well connected with his two jobs. She thrived, creating a haven for community knowledge and employment connections.

Grandma Mary Ellen was an incredible, strong, supportive role model for me growing up. She jumped in where needed and made the lives of everyone around richer while setting boundaries of home, marriage, children, extended family, neighbors, community, farmsteading, and profitability. She was surrogate grandma to all seven of her sibling's children and was upbeat about the future, no matter what was in store. As a child, I remember how she proudly hung her class photo from her high school class in her home for us all to see.

THE REALITY OF THE WORKING WOMAN IN MANUFACTURING

Throughout the entire time span of Mary Ellen's life, the role of the working women underwent massive change. However, some women entering the workplace did not fit into these regular norms and beliefs which were, and continue to be, well known and esteemed.

The first place where we truly saw women taking over jobs in manufacturing in the United States was during World War II. Women came to the rescue and entered the factories to keep the economy moving. Six million women entered the workplace during World War II. They felt betrayed when experiencing injustices, especially how skilled female coworkers were receiving $31.21 a week compared with men who earned $54.65 a week. Also, after the number of women in the workforce had jumped by from 27 percent in 1940 to 37 percent in 1945, when soldiers returned home and needed employment, they strongly urged women to let them have their jobs back. Consequently, in 1948, women in the US workforce dipped 4 percent to 32.7 percent.[318]

As some women were sent home after the men's return, the role of homemaker seemed lacking. Middle-class women left factories, but poor women continued in the workforce. Unfortunately, there are very few statistics of the women who worked during the 1950s and 1960s; they primarily worked not in factory jobs, but in retail and home services. Regardless, it was not a "perfect fit job."

Thankfully, some women had retained their jobs and continued to be the voice of women in the workplace. Their role was crucial as women reentered the workforce in droves from 1970s onward. As women moved up the corporate ladder, their presence was felt. In the following story, we find a woman whose career was a perfect fit for her.

THE MOST POWERFUL WOMAN IN THE COURTHOUSE— RUTH JANSSEN

When I was in grade school in the 1970s and 1980s, I had the great fortune of going to school near the local courthouse

318 Allison McNearney, "Watch Terrified Men Learn to Deal with Women in the Workforce During WWII," History Stories, updated May 5, 2018, accessed April 6, 2021.

where my father, a lawyer, tried court cases. On special days after school, my brother Pat and I would walk a few blocks to the Outagamie County Courthouse in Appleton to see him work. We knew we had to be well-behaved and abide by the special rules allotted to the justice system, yet the woman who ran the courthouse made our visits special, orderly, and fun. As we would walk into the pristine and somber courthouse building, we would visit the kind and all-so-knowledgeable clerk of courts, Ruth Janssen, who had been forewarned about our arrival by our father.

Ruth, in her role as clerk of courts, was in charge of establishing order in the four courtrooms, ensuring needed resources were available, and making sure the paperwork would be filed correctly from all of the day's court cases. She had a very big job!

Yet Ruth was not a lawyer. As a young woman, she had originally worked in the same office for her boss, another woman who was the clerk of courts. When her boss announced her retirement, my father, who was the district attorney at the time, encouraged Ruth to run for election to take over the position. My dad told her she knew how to do the job, was very personable, and was the best candidate. He became her campaign manager, and she ran against three candidates.

On election night, Ruth, my father, and the campaign staff went to a local bar called The Left Guard, owned by a Green Bay Packer who was the left guard, where the votes would be tallied. When the votes were counted, Ruth and my father waited alongside all of the candidates as the local radio station was called in to announce the winner. Around 11 p.m.

that evening, it was announced she had won the vote. Ruth was the new clerk of courts and held this position for over a decade. She set clear boundaries about respect for the law, the courthouse, and everyone who worked in it. She also respected herself to give herself time to do a good job. During her tenure, no one would ever run against her; she was the most qualified for the job.

BEING PROFESSIONAL ABOUT GROWTH IN A LEGAL BATTLE WITH MAYOR DOROTHY JOHNSON

As a preteen adolescent girl, I had the interesting opportunity of being amid a legal battle. Not a traumatic one, but one that was quite unique and pitted my father against the mayor. It was not just any mayor, but Appleton's first female mayor. Her name was Dorothy Johnson, and she was a married woman who was also a mother.

From shortly after her arrival in the mayor's office in 1980, she represented the city against the desire of developers to build a 330,000-square-foot, $25-million mall. Dorothy advocated for the needs of Appleton's local groups and environmentalists, who wanted to remain a vibrant city and opposed the building of this mall in Grand Chute, an adjacent town. Unfortunately, Dorothy and the city's needs conflicted with those of my family. We owned the land where the mall would be built, and our property became a hot topic. Dorothy and the city engaged in years of legal battles and my ten-year-old self was right in the middle of it.

Not only was the mall going to be built on my family's land, but the lawyer for the developer was my father. The mall and the controversy surrounding its development was a tense situation, and my friend's parents would heatedly tell me the pros and cons. To add fuel to the fire, I would listen as my dad would be interviewed on television, radio, or whatever medium was necessary defending the developers to ensure our city would not lose this opportunity to grow and become a viable economic engine in the state. Twice, the battle went before the Wisconsin State Supreme Court. When it won the second time, my father, who was also directing the contractors for the building of the mall, had the trucks on his property to begin the morning after the decision. National television cameras showed up to tell the public the story of how the Fox River Mall would be built after an intense legal battle.

What I learned over those years was how to be a professional: I had a woman as mayor to show me how, right alongside my father. After the losing the battle for special interest groups in Appleton, Dorothy demonstrated dignity even in defeat. She continued to listen to the needs of her stakeholders and advocate for them where needed. She did this while being farsighted enough to realize a change of heart was necessary to move forward and to ensure the long-term vision of creating a vibrant city would be realized.

As for my father, he treated Dorothy with respect while defending the needs of his clients, and he did so while explaining the news to my siblings and me. As the city and surrounding area listened in on the legal developments, Dorothy and my father taught me about the intricacies of conducting business professionally.

As a child, this experience was unique because I was proud of having a woman as a mayor, but I was also proud of my father. Truthfully, I really wanted a mall! The mall grew from sixty-seven stores at its inception to approximately 140 stores in 2020. The Fox River Mall's existence transformed our area into one of the largest growing parts of the state and helped Appleton thrive. In a way, Dorothy won too.

Dorothy was an excellent mayor who successfully served for three terms for twelve years. She set the clear boundaries of being a great mayor, a parent, and a key collaborator with those interesting in improving Appleton. She was a true professional and represented the city well.[319]

319 Maureen Wallenfang, "The Buzz: Fox River Mall turns 30," *The Post Crescent,* July 12, 2014.

Featured Stories
by Chapter

———

Here is a listing of where women fall in each chapter.

INTRODUCTION

- Amanda Baltz, Co-Founder & CEO of Spaulding Medical
- Kelly O'Brien, Career Management & Professional Development Coach

PART ONE: BREAKING THROUGH

CHAPTER ONE: BRUSQUE ENDINGS CREATE NEW PROFESSIONAL REALITIES

- Amanda Baltz, Co-Founder & CEO of Spaulding Medical
- Jackie Boynton, Founder of the Law Offices of Jacqueline Boynton
- Niki Kremer, CTA, VTA, Owner of Via Travel Service
- Thomas P. Leisle, Jr., Master Networker
- Lucy, Assertive Employee

CHAPTER TWO: THE AWESOME WOMEN INCUBATOR MODEL

- Jane Finette, Executive Director of The Coaching Fellowship
- Dr. J.J. Kelly, PysD, Founder of UnorthoDocs, Inc.
- Dave Vasko, Director of Research and Development at Rockwell Automation

CHAPTER THREE: THE INSPIRING OPPORTUNITY ENTREPRENEUR

- Amanda Baltz, Co-Founder & CEO of Spaulding Medical
- Dr. J.J. Kelly, PysD, Founder of UnorthoDocs, Inc.
- Sr. Kathleen Long, O.P., Peacemaker
- Anne Machesky, Founder & CEO of Nwyze Coaching Company

PART TWO: BREAKING AWAY

CHAPTER FOUR: THE BIRTH OF NECESSITY AND FLEXIBILITY ENTREPRENEURS

- Jacinda Ardern, Prime Minister of New Zeeland
- Elene Cafasso, President of Enerpace Inc Executive Coaching
- Maggie Cain, Owner at Three Wrens Boutique
- Carrie, Seeker of a Supportive Work Culture
- Waverly Deutsch, Clinical Professor of Entrepreneurship at The University of Chicago Booth School of Business
- Valerie Jarrett, Senior Adviser to President Obama & Chair of the White House Council on Women and Girls
- Savita Thakur Love, Strategic Initiatives Consultant & Aylianna and Deavon's Mom
- Cindy Machles, CEO of Glue Advertising and Public Relations

- Michelle Obama, Founder of The Michelle Obama Podcast
- Sheryl Sandberg, CEO at Facebook
- Phyllis Schlafly, Founder of STOP ERA
- Jamie Lynn Tatera, Founder of Wholly Mindful

CHAPTER FIVE: INSTITUTIONAL BETRAYAL IGNITES THE COURAGE WITHIN

- Ann Benjamin, Staff Director at WNET Thirteen
- Sara Larson, Founder & Executive Director of Awake Milwaukee
- Tanya Menon PhD, Professor at The Ohio State University
- Jen Schwartz, Founder of Therapeutic Massage by Jen
- Patty Trinko, Vice President of Program Development at Nwyze

CHAPTER SIX: MISFITS AWAKEN AND SIDEPRENEURS EMBARK

- Betty Jean Bartik, Creator of Modern-Day Software Engineering
- Eniac Six, Creators of Modern-Day Software Engineering
- Grace Hopper, Creator of Modern-Day Software Engineering
- Nadiyah Johnson, Founder of Milky Way Tech Hub & Jet Constellations
- Ada Lovelace, Creator of Computer Infrastructure
- Colleen McFarland, Author of *Disconnected: How to Use People Data to Deliver Realness, Meaning, and Belonging at Work*
- Rhonda, Women in the Midst of a Reinvention

- University of Wisconsin Milwaukee Lubar Entrepreneur-ship Center
- Amy Westrup, Legal Marketing Consultant & Improvisation Comedian and Coach

CHAPTER SEVEN: HOW AWESOME WOMEN CONFRONT SEXISM
- Kellie Freeze, Former Television Critic
- Jean Grow, Founder & Chief Truth Teller at GROW, a DEI Consultancy
- Mentoring Monday, Milwaukee Business Journal & American City Business Journals
- Suzanne, Real Estate Agent
- Thomas P. Leisle, Jr., Master Networker

PART THREE: BREAKING THE MOLD

CHAPTER EIGHT: COMBATTING THE MACRO EFFECTS OF MICRO-AGGRESSION
- Mary Burke, CEO & Founder of Building Brave
- Cindy Machles, CEO of Glue Advertising and Public Relations
- Alexandria Ocasio-Cortez, US Congresswoman
- Margarita Pineda-Ucero, Founder of Women Dignity Alliance
- Dave Vasko, Director of Research and Development at Rockwell Automation

CHAPTER NINE: POWERFUL NETWORKS PAVE THE WAY

- Ella L.J.E. Bell and Stella M. Nkomo, Authors of *Our Separate Ways: Black and White Women and the Struggle for Professional Identity*
- Jessica Bell, Inventor & Owner of Halo Vino
- Thomas P. Leisle, Jr., Master Networker
- Sharlen Moore, Founder of Urban Underground and Youth Justice Milwaukee
- On the Table, Greater Milwaukee Foundation

CHAPTER TEN: STOP ADVISING WOMEN TO GAIN CONFIDENCE

- Jane Finette, Executive Director of The Coaching Fellowship
- Jean Grow, Founder & Chief Truth Teller at GROW, a DEI Consultancy
- Anne Machesky, Founder & CEO of Nwyze Coaching Company
- Nancy Pelosi, Speaker of the House of Representatives, US Congress

CHAPTER ELEVEN: ENTREPRENEURS WHO INSPIRE US

- Hannah Anderson, Founder & Owner of Threepaws Gourmet
- Amanda Baltz, Co-Founder & CEO of Spaulding Medical
- Wendy K. Baumann, President/CVO of The Wisconsin Women's Business Initiative Corporation (WWBIC)
- Amy Gannon, Co-Founder of The Doyenne Group
- Cleise Gomes, Owner & Founder of Cleise Brazilian Day Spa
- Thomas P. Leisle, Jr., Master Networker

- Julia Taylor, President of the Greater Milwaukee Committee
- Heather Wentler, Co-Founder & Executive Director of The Doyenne Group

PART FOUR: TIPS AND TOOLS

STORIES FROM WOMEN WHO INSPIRED ME
- Ruth Janssen, Former Clerk of Courts, Outagamie County Courthouse
- Dorothy Johnson, Former Mayor of Appleton, Wisconsin
- Jim Long, Attorney at Law
- Mary Ellen Long, Hard Working Visionary

Recommended Resources

———

Now What? Where Do I Go from Here. You can access more information about how to move forward on your path at MalamaDoe's website on my author page. Find out more about the

Awesome Women Incubator Model
Wheel of Life
Business Model Canvas
Networking and Selling at Each Tier of the Model
Resources for Women's Equality

Acknowledgements

—

I'd like to thank the following individuals that supported my book by contributing to my pre-sale campaign. Their belief in all that Awesome Women can accomplish made this book possible:

Brian Acker, Anjum Alden, Molly Allen, Anita Bairoliya, Suzanne Baker, Amanda Baltz, Jennifer Barbieri, Carrie Baum, Annie Benjamin, Ashlee Berghoff, Meriem Boudjadja, Jen Burfeind, Mary Burke, Adam Burns, Andalis Burton, Frances Butler, Elene Cafasso, Maggie Cain, Alma Cerda, Adriana Cocozza, Katie Corcoran, PJ Coughlin, Rosemary Reilly Crawford, Dawn Davis, Nikki DeGuire, Ashley Dietrich, The Doyenne Group, Allison Duncan, Ruth Dwyer, Eric Eben, Liz Escobar, Amy Falluca, Leonore Faulds, Jane Finette, Anne Marie Finley, Tricia Geraghty, Melissa Lorek Ginter, Cleise Gomes, Nancy Granado, Dana Guthrie, Kristin Haglund, Mary Hannes, Gulnar Hasnain, Christel Henke, Anne Hildebrandt, Mary Louise Hildebrandt, Rebecca Holderness, Gina Jaeckel, Shar Jaegers, Diana Jakubowski, Cybil Joseph, Barbara Katzfey, Ryan Kauth, Pam Knauss, Eric Koester, Niki Kremer, Sara Larson, Megan Leadbetter,

Gillian Lester-George de Montesinos, James R Long, Kathleen Long, Kevin Long, Rita Long, Savita Thakur Love, Mary Beth LoVerdi, The Lubar Entrepreneurship Center, Pat Lucas, Jennifer Lulach, Anne Machesky, Cindy Machles, Kathleen Maguire, Beth Algiers Manley, Colleen McFarland, Laura McLaughlin, Seamus McNamara, Christine McQueen, Katie Meiers, Gregory K. Morris, Lisa Nelson, Carrie Neumann, Erin O'Donnell, Felisa Joy Parris, Julie Rabinowitz, Katie Reitman, Michele Reyes, Jennifer Rice, Roberta Richardson, Nora Rojas, Stan Rubin, Robert Ruff, Claudia Ryan, Maithili Sagar, Stephanie Salvia, Karen Schneider, Sarah Schneider, Lauren Schultz, Jennifer Schwartz, Annemarie Scobey, Eve Shalyaev, Irina Shleyfer, Courtney Skinkis, Michelle Skoien, Eileen Speidel, Sarah Spencer, Elizabeth Sumner, Cynthia Thomas, Three Paws Gourmet, Mai Ton, Patty Trinko, Vanessa Tsumura, Melanie Varin, Jennifer Verheyen, Laura Villamil, Carla Washington, Amy Westrup, Christine Wisdom, Women's Fund of Greater Milwaukee, Claudia Wright, and John Zidar.

I'd also like to thank the group of beta readers who've supported my campaign by giving feedback on my writing. Their insights shed light on what resonated and what did not and allowed for much richer content to be delivered in this book.

Anjum Alden, Hannah Anderson, Lisa Attonito, Amanda Baltz, Wendy K. Baumann, Annie Benjamin, Ashlee Berghoff, Meriem Boudjadja, Jackie Boynton, Mary Burke, Frances Butler, Elene Cafasso, Maggie Cain, Victor A. Cain, Dawn Davis, Denise Dilley, Waverly Deutsch, Liz Escobar, Jane Finette, Anne Marie Finley, Kelly Freeze, Cleise Gomes, Becky Grandone, Jean Grow, Dana Guthrie, Therese Heeg,

Christel Henke, Anne Hildebrandt, Mary Louise Hildebrandt, Rhonda Hill, Gina Jaeckel, Diana Jakubowski, Nadiyah Johnson, Barbara Katzfey, Ryan Kauth, TK Kingston, Niki Kremer, Sara Larson, James R Long, Kathleen Long, Kevin Long, Rita Long, Savita Thakur Love, Anne Machesky, Cindy Machles, Colleen McFarland, Cary McIlvoy, Laura McLaughlin, Katie Meiers, Sharlen Moore, Felisa Joy Parris, Margarita Pineda-Ucera, Julie Rabinowitz, Robert Ruff, Jennifer Schwartz, Michelle Sherbinow, Irina Shleyfer, Eileen Speidel, Nathaniel Stern, Lisa Sullivan, Elizabeth Sumner, Julia Taylor, Cynthia Thomas, Patty Trinko, Vicki Updike, Dave Vasko, Jennifer Verheyen, Carla Washington, Heather Wentler, Amy Westrup, and Claudia Wright.

Special thanks go out to Nathaniel Stern of the UWM Lubar Entreprenuership Center for encouraging me to publish my work. I am grateful for the help of my sister and fellow author Colleen McFarland, who connected me to the entire editing team at New Degree Press, including our fearless leaders Eric Koester and Brian Bies.

I would like to thank my Developmental Editor, Quinn Karrenbauer, for encouraging me to see the light at the end of the tunnel. Sorting through an incredible amount of information was quite overwhelming, and she was instrumental in prioritizing how to best tell the story. With her key insights, I delved into the important issues, then created and recreated chapter lists, and produced a written manuscript that resonated.

My Revisions Editor, Chelsea Olivia, cheerfully guided me along as we converted the first manuscript into this book through multiple rounds of revisions. While working on the pre-sale campaign, incorporating beta reader feedback, and working through citations, her desire to artfully and accurately tell the stories of these courageous women was instrumental and much appreciated. Her insights into the struggles women face and the importance of how authors give voice to them by "opening the door" for the reader were key in my developing the content in this book.

Both Quinn and Chelsea's ability to see the value of telling the stories made the book come to life. I thank them both for seeing the value in sharing women's life lessons.

I would additionally like thank my Advisory Council from MalamaDoe for their support over the years, especially Heather Thomas Flores, Heather Wentler, Robert DeVita, Lisa Attonito, Thalia Mendez, Jason Stansell, and Kevin Long.

Most importantly, I would like to thank my three children. They have patiently supported me as I launched a business and joyfully cheered me on as I wrote this book during the COVID-19 pandemic.

Appendix

—

INTRODUCTION

American Express. *The 2019 State of Women-Owned Business Report*. New York: American Express, 2019. https://s1.q4cdn.com/692158879/files/doc_library/file/2019-state-of-women-owned-businesses-report.pdf.

Ewing Marion Kauffman Foundation. "Historical Kauffman Index." Accessed January 15, 2021. https://www.kauffman.org/historical-kauffman-index/.

Harper's Bazaar. "60 Empowering Feminist Quotes from Inspiring Women." February 28, 2020. https://www.harpersbazaar.com/culture/features/a4056/empowering-female-quotes/.

Lesonsky, Rieva. "The State of Women Entrepreneurs." *Score (blog)*, March 24, 2020. https://www.score.org/blog/state-women-entrepreneurs.

MalamaDoe. "Our Story." Accessed March 29, 2021. https://malamadoe.com/our-story/.

Ortiz-Ospina, Esteban and Diana Beltekian. "Why Do Women Live Longer Than Men?" *Our World in Data* (blog), August 14, 2018. Accessed March 27, 2021. https://ourworldindata.org/why-do-women-live-longer-than-men.

Stengel, Geri. "How Women Entrepreneurs Are Redefining Wealth Management." *Forbes*, March 27, 2019. https://www.forbes.com/sites/geristengel/2019/03/27/how-women-entrepreneurs-are-redefining-managing-their-wealth/.

Stonjanovic, Andrea. "Ladies who Lead - 35+ Amazing Women in Business Statistics." *Small Biz Genius*(blog), December 2, 2020. Accessed March 27, 2021. https://www.smallbizgenius.net/by-the-numbers/women-in-business-statistics/#gref.

U.S. Small Business Administration Office of Advocacy. "United States Small Business Report. 2019." Washington DC: U.S. Small Business Administration, 2019. Accessed March 26, 2021. https://cdn.advocacy.sba.gov/wp-content/uploads/2019/04/23142719/2019-Small-Business-Profiles-US.pdf.

Vuleta, Branka. "22 Mind-Blowing Women Entrepreneurs Statistics." *What To Become* (blog), August, 11, 2020. https://whattobecome.com/blog/women-entrepreneurs-statistics/.

CHAPTER ONE

Bartolomé, Fernando and Paul A. Lee Evans. "Why Must Success Cost So Much?" *Harvard Business Review*, March 1980. https://hbr.org/1980/03/must-success-cost-so-much.

Bergeron, Ryan. "'The Seventies': Feminism Makes Waves." *CNN,* August 17, 2015. https://www.cnn.com/2015/07/22/living/the-seventies-feminism-womens-lib/index.html.

Chang, Emily. *Brotopia: Breaking up the Boys' Club of Silicon Valley.* New York: Penguin Audio, 2018. Audible audio ed. 6 hr., 53 min.

Emily's List. "Home." Accessed February 6, 2021. https://www.emilyslist.org/.

Enerpace. "Meet Our Team." Accessed March 27, 2021. https://www.enerpace.com/meet-our-team.

Fins, Amanda. *Women and the Lifetime Wage Gap: How Many Woman Years Does It Take To Equal 40 Man Years?* Washington, D.C.: National Women's Law Center, 2020. https://nwlc-ciw-49tixgw5lbab.stackpathdns.com/wp-content/uploads/2020/03/Women-and-the-Lifetime-Wage-Gap.pdf.

Polsky Center for Entrepreneurship & Innovation. "Home." The University of Chicago. Accessed February 6, 2021. https://polsky.uchicago.edu/.

Stebbins, Samuel and Thomas C. Frohlich. "20 Jobs with the Largest Gender Pay Gap for Women." *USA Today,* December 5, 2018. https://www.usatoday.com/story/money/careers/2018/12/05/gender-pay-gap-2018-worst-paying-jobs-women/38565069/.

Stieg, Cory. "How the Gender Pay Gap Affects Women's Mental Health." *CNBC,* March 31, 2020. https://www.cnbc.com/2020/03/31/how-the-gender-pay-gap-affects-womens-mental-health.html.

The University of Chicago Booth School of Business. "Home." Accessed February 6, 2021. https://www.chicagobooth.edu/.

Via Travel Service. "About." Accessed February 6, 2021. https://www.viatravelservice.com/about-me.

Wholly Mindful. "Jamie Lynn's Story and Training: Meet Jamie Lynn." About us. Accessed March 28, 2021. https://www.whollymindful.com/jamie-lynns-story-and-training.html.

Wilcox, W. Bradford. "The Evolution of Divorce." *National Affairs*, Fall 2009. https://www.nationalaffairs.com/publications/detail/the-evolution-of-divorce.

Women Lead Wisconsin. "Home." Accessed February 6, 2021. http://www.womenleadwi.org/.

CHAPTER TWO

Dr. Kristin Neff. "Tips for Practice." Practices. Self-Compassion. Accessed February 13, 2021. https://self-compassion.org/tips-for-practice.

Goldman Sachs. *Voice of Small Business in America: 2019 Insights Report.* New York: Goldman Sachs, 2019. https://www.goldmansachs.com/citizenship/10000-small-businesses/US/2019-insights-report/report.pdf.

MalamaDoe. "Book by Sheila Long." Accessed April 7, 2021. https://malamadoe.com/sheilalongauthor/.

McLaughlin, Elizabeth. "The Heroine's Journey: Betrayal." Gaia Leadership Project. Accessed February 8, 2021. https//gaialeadershipproject.com/theheroinesjourneybetrayal/.

Score. "The Megaphone of Main Street: Women's Entrepreneurship, Infographic #4: How and Why Women Start Businesses." November 5, 2018. Accessed March 27, 2021. https://www.score.org/resource/infographic/megaphone-main-street-how-why-women-start-businesses.

University of Wisconsin Milwaukee. "Our Community." Lubar Entrepreneurship Center. Accessed March 20, 2021. https://uwm.edu/lubar-entrepreneurship-center/community/.

Yousafzai, Malala. "Malala Yousafzai." *Explainers* (blog). *Their World,* July 12, 2013. Accessed February 8, 2021. https://their-world.org/explainers/malala-yousafzais-speech-at-the-youth-takeover-of-the-united-nations.

CHAPTER THREE

American Express. *The 2019 State of Women-Owned Business Report.* New York: American Express, 2019. https://s1.q4cdn.com/692158879/files/doc_library/file/2019-state-of-women-owned-businesses-report.pdf.

Archdiocese of Chicago. "Archdiocese of Chicago Celebrates 18th Annual Noche de Gala with Theme 'Celebrating the Extraordinary Jubilee of Mercy'." Archdiocese of Chicago news release, September 27, 2016. Archdiocese of Chicago website. Accessed April 12, 2021. https://www.archchicago.org/news-releases/-/asset_publisher/lge4tDy8ErBD/content/

news-release-archdiocese-of-chicago-celebrates-18th-an-
nual-noche-de-gala-with-theme-celebrating-the-extraordi-
nary-jubilee-of-mercy-?inheritRedirect=false.

Kelly, J.J. "About J.J." Accessed January 22, 2021. https://www.drjj-
kelly.com/about.

Kelly, J.J. "How about we shoot a little higher, toward joy instead
of just existing?" Facebook, January 9, 2021. Accessed
March 31, 2021. https://www.facebook.com/Dr.JJKelly/pho-
tos/a.380068285917947/797742410817197.

Kelly PsyD., J.J. *Holy Shit, I'm A Gifted "Misfit!:" The Young Folx
Guide to Unlock Your Superpower.* Oakland: Independently
published, 2020.

Kelly PsyD., J.J. *Holy Sh*t, My Kid Is Cutting: The Complete Plan
to Stop Self Harm.* Washington D.C.: Difference Press, 2020.

Kurowski, Jeff. "Appleton Nun Arrested in Protest." *The Compass,* December 6, 2002. Accessed January 18, 2021. https://
www.thecompassnews.org/compass/2002-12-06/02cn1206l3.
shtml.

Nwyze. "Home." Accessed March 31, 2021. http://www.nwyze.com/.

Reed, Athea and Diane Dixon. *Financial Services: Women at the
Top. A Woman in Insurance and Financial Services Research
Study.* Indiana: iUniverse, July 31, 2015.

Salgado, Soli. "Q&A with SR. Kathleen Long, Helping Immigrants
Become U.S. Citizens." *Global Sisters Report* (blog), September

28, 2016. Accessed April 10, 2021. https://www.globalsistersre-
port.org/blog/q/ministry/q-sr-kathleen-long-helping-immi-
grants-become-us-citizens-42481.

Score. "The Megaphone of Main Street: Women's Entrepreneurship, Infographic #4: How and Why Women Start Businesses."
November 5, 2018. Accessed March 27, 2021. https://www.score.
org/resource/infographic/megaphone-main-street-how-why-
women-start-businesses.

Spaulding Clinical. "Home." Accessed March 31, 2021. http://www.
spauldingclinical.com.

Vuleta, Branka. "22 Mind-Blowing Women Entrepreneurs Statistics." *What To Become* (blog), August 11, 2020. https://whatto-
become.com/blog/women-entrepreneurs-statistics/.

CHAPTER FOUR

Aaron, Margo. "These Women Prove That Having Kids Makes
You a Better Business Owner, Not a Worse One." *Mother Hustle* (blog), April 10, 2018. Accessed March 21, 2021. http://www.
motherhustle.com/women-prove-kids-makes-better-business-
owner-not-worse-one/.

Adams, Susan. "10 Things Sheryl Sandberg Gets Exactly Right in
'Lean In'." *Forbes,* March 4, 2013. Accessed February 14, 2021.
https://www.forbes.com/sites/susanadams/2013/03/04/10-things-
sheryl-sandberg-gets-exactly-right-in-lean-in/?sh=79a7747a7ada.

Bartolomé, Fernando and Paul A. Lee Evans. "Why Must Success Cost So Much." *Harvard Business Review*, March 1980. https://hbr.org/1980/03/must-success-cost-so-much.

Boesch, Diana and Katie Hamm. *Valuing Women's Caregiving During and After the Coronavirus Crisis.* Washington DC: Center for American Progress, 2020. https://www.american-progress.org/issues/women/reports/2020/06/03/485855/valuing-womens-caregiving-coronavirus-crisis/.

Cafasso, Elene. "A Balanced Life: What Is It?" *Enerpace, Inc. (blog),* December 2, 2020. Accessed February 8, 2021. https://www.enerpace.com/a-balanced-life-what-is-it/.

Caprino, Kathy. "How Decision-Making Is Different between Men and Women and Why It Matters in Business." *Forbes,* May 12, 2016. Accessed February 13, 2021. https://www.forbes.com/sites/kathycaprino/2016/05/12/how-decision-making-is-different-between-men-and-women-and-why-it-matters-in-business/?sh=6bd2900a4dcd.

Chamorro-Premuzic, Tomás. "Why Do So Many Incompetent Men Become Leaders?" *Harvard Business Review,* August 22, 2013. Accessed March 20, 2021. https://hbr.org/2013/08/why-do-so-many-incompetent-men?utm_medium=social&utm_campaign=hbr&utm_source=linkedin&tpcc=orgsocial_edit.

Chicago Booth. "Booth Women Connect." Accessed March 28, 2021. https://www.chicagobooth.edu/booth-women-connect.

Cohen, Alex and Wilfred U. Codrington III. "The Equal Rights Amendment Explained." Our Work, Research & Reports, *Bren-*

nan *Center for Justice,* January 23, 2020. Accessed February 9, 2021. https://www.brennancenter.org/our-work/research-reports/equal-rights-amendment-explained.

Derbyshire, Victoria. "New Zealand PM Jacinda Ardern: 'I'm a Mother, Not a Superwoman." Produced by *BBC Two* and *BBC News.* Featuring Jacinda Ardern. London: *BBC.* January 21, 2019. Video, 1:42. https://www.bbc.com/news/av/world-46949772.

Deutsch, Waverly. "Women in Entrepreneurship: The Story Behind the Data." Powerpoint presentation at the 5th Annual Booth Women Connect Conference, The University of Chicago Booth School of Business Booth Women Connect, Chicago, IL, October 23, 2015.

ERA Coalition. "About the Coalition." Accessed March 28, 2021. http://www.eracoalition.org/about.

ERA Coalition. "Home." Accessed March 28, 2021. http://www.eracoalition.org/.

Felsenthal, Carol. *Phyllis Schlafly; the Sweetheart of the Silent Majority.* Washington D.C.: Regnery Gateway, 1982.

Glue Advertising. "About." Accessed February 18, 2021. https://www.glueadvertising.com.

Graham-McLay, Charlotte. "Jacinda Ardern Embraces Dual Role: New Zealand Prime Minister and Mom." *New York Times,* updated August 2, 2018. Accessed April 9, 2021. https://www.nytimes.com/2018/08/02/world/asia/jacinda-ardern-maternity-leave-new-zealand.html.

Institute on Aging. "Aging in America." Education. Accessed March 28, 2021. https://www.ioaging.org/aging-in-america.

Jarrett, Valerie. "Valerie Jarrett on 26-Year-Old Michelle Obama's Unforgettable Job Interview." *Literary Hub*, April 4th, 2019. Accessed February 14, 2021. https://lithub.com/valerie-jarrett-on-26-year-old-michelle-obamas-unforgettable-job-interview/.

Jones, Eileen. "There's Nothing Good about Phyllis Schlafly." *Jacobin Mag*, May 20, 2020. https://jacobinmag.com/2020/05/mrs-america-series-review-phyllis-schlafly.

Kennedy, Lesley. "How Phyllis Schlafly Derailed the Equal Rights Amendment." *History.com*, March 19, 2020. Accessed February 9, 2021. https://www.history.com/news/equal-rights-amendment-failure-phyllis-schlafly.

Lean In. "Lean In Circles." Accessed February 14, 2021. https://leanin.org/circles#!.

Madowitz, Michael and Alex Rowell, and Katie Hamm. *Calculating the Hidden Cost of Interrupting a Career for Child Care*. Washington DC: Center for American Progress, 2016. https://www.americanprogress.org/issues/early-childhood/reports/2016/06/21/139731/calculating-the-hidden-cost-of-interrupting-a-career-for-child-care/.

MalamaDoe. "Book by Sheila Long." Accessed April 7, 2021. https://malamadoe.com/sheilalongauthor/.

Martin, Douglas. "Phyllis Schlafly, 'First Lady' of a Political March to the Right, Dies at 92." *New York Times*, September 5, 2016.

https://www.nytimes.com/2016/09/06/obituaries/phyllis-schla-fly-conservative-leader-and-foe-of-era-dies-at-92.html.

NAC and AARP Public Policy Institute. *2015 Report: Caregiving in the U.S. National Alliance for Caregiving and AARP Public Policy Institute.* Washington D.C.: NAC and AARP Public Policy Institute, 2015. https://www.aarp.org/content/dam/aarp/ppi/2015/caregiving-in-the-united-states-2015-report-revised.pdf.

Obama, Michelle, Valerie Jarrett, Dan Fierman, Anna Holmes, and Mukta Mohan. "Working Women: Valerie Jarrett and the Importance of Mentorship." September 30, 2020. In *The Michelle Obama Podcast.* Produced by Higher Ground Audio. Podcast, MP3 audio, 44:20. https://storage.googleapis.com/pr-news-room-wp/1/2020/09/TMOP-Transcript_Ep-7-Pt1_Mentors.pdf.

Roy, Eleanore Ainge. "Jacinda Ardern Makes History with Baby Neve at UN General Assembly." *The Guardian,* September 24, 2018. Accessed February 14, 2021. https://www.theguardian.com/world/2018/sep/25/jacinda-ardern-makes-history-with-baby-neve-at-un-general-assembly.

Sandberg, Sheryl. *Lean In: Women, Work and the Will to Lead.* New York: Knopf, 2013.

Sandberg, Sheryl. "Why We Have Too Few Women Leaders." Filmed December 2010 in Washington, D.C. TED video, 14:42. https://www.ted.com/talks/sheryl_sandberg_why_we_have_too_few_women_leaders?language=en#t-66805.

Schlafly, Phyllis. *The Power of the Positive Woman.* New York City: Crown Pub, 1977.

Seligson, Hannah. "Nurturing a Baby and a Start-up Business." *New York Times*, June 9, 2012. Accessed March 21, 2021. https://www.nytimes.com/2012/06/10/business/nurturing-a-baby-and-a-start-up-business.html.

Three Wrens. "About Us." Accessed March 28, 2021. https://www.threewrensboutique.com/pages/about-us.

University of Chicago Booth School of Business. "Booth Women Connect 2015. Women in Entrepreneurship: The Story Behind the Data. Professor Waverly Deutsch." Facebook, November 11, 2015. https://www.facebook.com/chicagoboothbusiness/photos/a.10156224263185402/10156224264370402.

Wholly Mindful. "Jamie Lynn's Story and Training: Meet Jamie Lynn." About us. Accessed March 28, 2021. https://www.whollymindful.com/jamie-lynns-story-and-training.html.

Winter, Dayna. "9 Businesses Run by Badass Multitasking Supermoms." *Shopify (blog)*, May 12, 2017. Accessed March 21, 2021. https://www.shopify.com/blog/117043653-10-businesses-run-by-badass-multitasking-super-moms-giveaway.

Woolley, Anita and Thomas W. Malone. "Defend Your Research: What Makes a Team Smarter? More Women." *Harvard Business Review,* June 2011. https://hbr.org/2011/06/defend-your-research-what-makes-a-team-smarter-more-women.

CHAPTER FIVE

ABC News. "Home." Accessed February 6, 2021. https://abcnews.go.com/.

Awake Milwaukee. "Home." Accessed April 5, 2021. https://awake-milwaukee.org.

Awake Milwaukee. "Leadership." Who We Are. Awake Milwaukee. Accessed March 2, 2021. https://awakemilwaukee.org/leadership/.

Awake Milwaukee. "Sign Awake's Open Letter to Survivors." The Letter. Accessed April 5, 2021. https://awakemilwaukee.org/theletter/.

Center for Institutional Courage. "Knowledge Base and Research Priorities." Accessed March 28, 2021. https://www.institutionalcourage.org/knowledge-base-and-research-priorities.

Directors Guild of America. "Live from the Control Room: Ann Benjamin." Produced by Directors Guild of America. *Directors Guild of America,* September 27, 2018. Video, 1:02. Accessed February 6, 2021. https://www.dga.org/VideoHTMLNew.ashx-?id=%7B65E6A28C-026D-4E2C-997A-BE288861AB76%7D&db=web.

Directors Guild of America. "Live from the Control Room: News Directors in Conversation." Events. Directors Guild of America. September 27, 2018. Accessed February 6, 2021. https://www.dga.org/Events/2018/Nov2018/FOW_DirectingNetworkNews.aspx.

Fortune. "Fortune 500." Accessed January 28, 2020. https://fortune.com/fortune500/#.

Freyd, Jennifer and Pamela Birrell. *Blind to Betrayal: Why We Fool Ourselves We Aren't Being Fooled.* Hoboken: Wiley, 2013.

Freyd, PhD., Jennifer J. "Research." Accessed February 6, 2021. https://www.jjfreyd.com/about-research.

Globokar, Lidjia. "What Are Women Most Afraid Of?" *Forbes,* March 8, 2019. Accessed March 28, 2021. https://www.forbes.com/sites/lidijaglobokar/2019/03/08/what-are-women-most-afraid-of/?sh=d84d8877b8b1.

Jones, Erica. "Clergy Sexual Abuse Cases Still Rising." *Urban Milwaukee,* November 17, 2019. Accessed February 7, 2021. https://urbanmilwaukee.com/2019/11/17/catholic-clergy-abuse-clergy-sexual-abuse-cases-still-rising/.

McLaughlin, Elizabeth. "The Heroine's Journey: Betrayal." Gaia Leadership Project. Accessed February 8, 2021. https//gaialeadershipproject.com/theheroinesjourneybetrayal/.

Menon, Tanya. "Women in Business: You're a Threat, Own It!" Powerpoint Presentation at the 5th Annual Booth Women Connect Conference, Booth Women Connect, Chicago, IL. October 23, 2015.

O'Donnell, Erin. "5 Ways the Catholic Church Can Build More 'Institutional Courage'." *Awake Milwaukee* (blog), September 30, 2020. Accessed February 7, 2021. https://awakemilwaukee.org/2020/09/30/5-ways-the-catholic-church-can-build-more-institutional-courage/.

PBS. "Home." Accessed February 6, 2021. https://www.pbs.org/.

Tan, Jo-Ann. "For Women of Color, the Glass Ceiling is Actually Made of Concrete." *HuffPost (blog),* April 20, 2016. https://www. huffpost.com/entry/for-women-of-color-the-gl_b_9728056.

Therapeutic Massage by Jen, LLC. "Now Booking Appointments." Facebook, July 19, 2020. Accessed February 7, 2021. https://www.facebook.com/Therapeutic-Massage-by-Jen-LLC-109183124210082.

Thomas, Lauren. "The Retail Industry Is Leading the Way as Women Take over CEO Roles." *CNBC,* December 28, 2020. Accessed January 28, 2020. https://www.cnbc.com/2020/12/28/the-retail-industry-is-leading-the-way-as-women-take-over-ceo-roles.html.

The University of Chicago Booth School of Business. "Booth Women Connect." Booth Women Connect. Accessed March 28, 2021. https://www.chicagobooth.edu/booth-women-connect.

Trinko, Patty. Email message to author. August 24, 2020.

WNET Thirteen. "Home." Accessed February 6, 2021. https://www. thirteen.org/.

Zimmer, Ben. "The Phrase 'Glass Ceiling' Stretches Back Decades." *The Wall Street Journal,* April 3, 2015. Accessed January 24, 2021. https://www.wsj.com/articles/the-phrase-glass-ceiling-stretches-back-decades-1428089010.

CHAPTER SIX

Anderegg, Brandon. "Milky Way Tech Hub to Launch $50 Million Fund to Invest In Tech Companies Owned By Minorities." *BizTimes*, June 24, 2020. Accessed April 12, 2021. https://biztimes.com/milky-way-tech-hub-to-launch-50-million-fund-to-invest-in-tech-companies-owned-by-minorities/.

Bartolomé, Fernando and Paul A. Lee Evans. "Why Must Success Cost So Much." *Harvard Business Review*, March 1980. https://hbr.org/1980/03/must-success-cost-so-much.

Buchanan, Robert Angus. "History of Technology." *Encyclopedia Britannica,* November 18, 2020. Accessed March 23, 2021. https://www.britannica.com/technology/history-of-technology.

CareerBuilder. "Nearly Three in Four Employers Affected by a Bad Hire, According to a Recent CareerBuilder Survey." CareerBuilder press release, December 7, 2017. CareerBuilder website. Accessed April 4, 2021. https://press.careerbuilder.com/2017-12-07-Nearly-Three-in-Four-Employers-Affected-by-a-Bad-Hire-According-to-a-Recent-CareerBuilder-Survey.

Chang, Emily. *Brotopia: Breaking up the Boys' Club of Silicon Valley.* New York: Penguin Audio, 2018. Audible audio ed., 37 min and 1 hr., 21 min.

Coleman, Alison. "Six Technology Trends That Will Shape Businesses in 2020." *Forbes,* Feb 4, 2020. https://www.forbes.com/sites/alisoncoleman/2020/02/04/six-technology-trends-that-will-shape-businesses-in-2020/?sh=6a35f4a2105e.

Comedy Sportz. "CSZ Applied Improv." Private Events. Accessed January 24, 2021. http://www.cszmke.com/appliedimprov.

Eniac Programmers. "Home." Accessed March 23, 2021. http://eniacprogrammers.org/.

Evans, Claire L. *Broad Band: The Untold Story of the Women Who Made the Internet. New York:* Portfolio Penguin, 2018. Kindle.

History of Scientific Women. "Grace Hopper." Accessed March 23, 2021. https://scientificwomen.net/women/hopper-grace-45.

Jet Constellations. "Home." Accessed January 24, 2021. https://jetconstellations.com/.

Johnson, Nadiyah. "BIT TechTalk ep. 121 w/ Nadiyah Johnson of Jet Constellations." June 2, 2020. In *Tech Talk Blacks in Technology.* Produced by Blacks in Technology. Podcast, MP3 audio, 60:32. https://www.blacksintechnology.net/bittechtalk-ep-121-w-nadiyah-johnson/.

Johnson, Nadiyah. "Episode 11 — The Young Shall Lead Them - Host Jordan Davis." November 3, 2019. In *Down to Mars Podcast.* Produced by Nadiyah Johnson. Podcast, MP3 audio, 23:35. https://anchor.fm/downtomarsmke/episodes/Episode-11----The-Young-Shall-Lead-Them---Host-Jordan-Davis-e8msb0.

Johnson, Nadiyah. "Stars Tell a Story." Filmed October 2020 at TEDxMarquetteU in Milwaukee, WI. Video, 15:01. https://www.ted.com/talks/nidiyah_johnson_stars_tell_a_story.

Kroeker, Kirk L. "Remembering Jean Bartik." *ACM News,* April 19, 2011. Accessed March 23, 2021. https://cacm.acm.org/news/107514-remembering-jean-bartik/fulltext.

MalamaDoe. "Book by Sheila Long." Accessed April 7, 2021. https://malamadoe.com/sheilalongauthor/.

McClendon, Kiara. "The Crown Act Makes Waves across the Country to End Hair Discrimination." *Forbes*, January 13, 2021. Accessed March 23, 2021. https://www.forbes.com/sites/forbes-theculture/2021/01/13/the-crown-act-makes-waves-across-the-country-to-end-hair-discrimination/?sh=5cb47d14eb5a.

McFarland, Colleen. *Disconnected: How to Use People Data to Deliver Realness, Meaning, and Belonging at Work*. Potomac: New Degree Press. 2020.

Meekins, Carole. "Milwaukee Woman Works to Expand Tech Opportunities in the City." Positively Milwaukee. *TMJ4*, May 3, 2019. Accessed January 24, 2021. https://www.tmj4.com/news/positively-milwaukee/milwaukee-woman-works-to-expand-tech-opportunities-in-the-city.

Shaw, Bianca. "Founder of Milky Way Tech Hub Meets Vice President Kamala Harris on Second Day in Office." *Milky Way Tech Hub (blog)*, January 24, 2021. Accessed April 4, 2021. https://milkywaytechhub.com/founder-of-milky-way-tech-hub-meets-with-vice-president-kamala-harris-on-second-day-in-office/.

Strategyzer. "What is a Business Model?" Accessed April 4, 2021. https://www.strategyzer.com/expertise/business-models.

Sturt, David. "3 Ways to Weed Out a Bad Job Candidate: Don't make another bad hire ever again." *Fortune Insiders (blog)*. *Medium*, September 16, 2013. https://insiders.fortune.com/3-ways-to-weed-out-a-bad-job-candidate-ee365294c331.

The Crown Act. "Home." Accessed March 23, 2021. https://www.thecrownact.com/.

WisPolitics. "Biden Campaign: Following Kamala Harris' Visit, Milwaukee Black Business Owners Praise Build Back Better Plan." WisPolitics press release, September 9, 2020. WisPolitics website. Accessed April 4, 2021. https://www.wispolitics.com/2020/biden-campaign-following-kamala-harris-visit-milwaukee-black-business-owners-praise-build-back-better-plan/.

CHAPTER SEVEN

Adams, Susan. "When the Boss Hits on You." *Forbes*, June 25, 2013. https://www.forbes.com/sites/susanadams/2013/06/25/when-the-boss-hits-on-you-3/?sh=ce7333d5cd87.

BBC News. "Ruth Bader Ginsburg in Pictures and Her Own Words." September 19, 2020. Accessed January 16, 2020. https://www.bbc.com/news/world-us-canada-54218139.

Fine, Jerramy. *In Defense of the Princess: How Plastic Tiaras and Fairytale Dreams Can Inspire Smart, Strong Women*. Philadelphia: Running Press Adult, 2016.

Freyd, PhD., Jennifer J. "Research." Accessed February 6, 2021. https://www.jjfreyd.com/about-research.

Kass, Mark. "Speed Coaching — Mentoring Monday Draws Big Crowd: Slideshow." *Milwaukee Business Journal,* updated on April 3, 2017. Accessed January 18, 2020. https://www.bizjournals.com/milwaukee/news/2017/04/03/speed-coaching-mentoring-monday-draws-big-crowd.html.

Mikkelson, David. "Did These Words Originate with Ruth Bader Ginsberg?" Fact Check. Snopes. September 24, 2020. Accessed March 6, 2021. https://www.snopes.com/fact-check/rbg-brethren-quote/.

Sandberg, Sheryl. *Lean in: Women, Work and the Will to Lead.* New York: Knopf, 2013.

Sattari, Negin, Emily Shaffer, PhD., Sarah DiMuccio, and Dnika J. Travis, PhD. "Interrupting Sexism at Work: What Drives Men to Respond Directly or Do Nothing?" *Catalyst,* June 25, 2020. https://www.catalyst.org/reports/interrupting-sexism-workplace-men/.

Times Up. "About." Accessed March 25, 2021. https://timesupnow.org/about/.

Tour of America's Dairyland. "Schedule." Accessed March 25,2021. https://www.tourofamericasdairyland.com/schedule/.

CHAPTER EIGHT

Alter, Charlotte. "'Change Is Closer Than We Think.' Inside Alexandria Ocasio-Cortez's Unlikely Rise." *Time,* March 21, 2019. Accessed February 20, 2021. https://time.com/longform/alexandria-ocasio-cortez-profile.

Archer, Adelle and Alexandra Cole, Alexandra Suhner Isenberg, Adeline Desjonqueres, Alllson Byers, Amanda Shine, Billur Karamanci et al. "Cindy Machles." *Founded by Women: Inspiration and Advice from over 100 Female Founders*. San Francisco: Databird Business Journal, 2021.

Beekman, Daniel. "Diverse Group of Startups Thriving at City-Sponsored Sunshine Bronx Business Incubator in Hunts Point." *New York Daily News,* July 17, 2012. Accessed April 5, 2021. https://www.nydailynews.com/new-york/bronx/diverse-group-startups-thriving-city-sponsored-sunshine-bronx-business-incubator-hunts-point-article-1.1115489.

Broadwater, Luke and Catie Edmondson. "A.O.C. Unleashes a Viral Condemnation of Sexism in Congress." *New York Times,* July 23, 2020. Accessed February 20, 2021. https://www.nytimes.com/2020/07/23/us/alexandria-ocasio-cortez-sexism-congress.html?auth=login-email&login=email.

Building Brave. "Home." Accessed February 16, 2021. https://www.buildingbrave.org/.

Congresswoman Alexandria Cortez. "Biography." About. Accessed April 5, 2021. https://ocasio-cortez.house.gov/about/biography.

Evelyn, Kenya. "Alexandria Ocasio-Cortez Thought She 'Was Going to Die' during Capitol Attack." *The Guardian,* January 13, 2021. https://www.theguardian.com/us-news/2021/jan/13/alexandria-ocasio-cortez-aoc-capitol-attack-instagram-live-video.

Expertise.com. "We Scored 1,214 Advertising Agencies in New York, NY and Picked the Top 36." Business Services. Accessed

February 19, 2021. https://www.expertise.com/ny/nyc/advertising-agencies.

Founded by Women. "Cindy Machles." Contributors. Accessed February 20, 2021. https://www.foundedbywomen.org/contributors/cindy-machles.

Glue Advertising. "About." Accessed February 18, 2021. https//www.glueadvertising.com/#about.

Glueck, Katie. "Ocasio-Cortez Says She Is a Sexual Assault Survivor." *New York Times*, February 1, 2021. Accessed April 5, 2021. https://www.nytimes.com/2021/02/01/nyregion/aoc-sexual-assault-abuse.html.

Grantham-Phillips, Wyatt and Jessica Flores. "'The Squad' Stays Strong: Alexandria Ocasio-Cortez, Ilhan Omar, Ayanna Pressley and Rashida Tlaib Win Reelection." *USA Today,* November 4, 2020. Accessed February 18, 2021. https://www.usatoday.com/story/news/politics/elections/2020/11/04/aoc-ilhan-omar-ayanna-pressley-rashida-tlaib-squad-wins/6156013002/.

Jean-Philippe, McKenzie. "4 Quick Facts to Know about Alexandria Ocasio-Cortez." *Oprah Daily,* August 19, 2020. https://www.oprahdaily.com/entertainment/tv-movies/a33637079/who-is-alexandria-ocasio-cortez/.

Jones, Kenneth and Tema Okun. "Ladder of Empowerment." In *Dismantling Racism 2016 Workbook*. Durham: dR works, 2016. Accessed February 20, 2021. https://resourcegeneration.org/wp-content/uploads/2018/01/2016-dRworks-workbook.pdf.

Kivel, Paul. *White People's Resistance, Uprooting Racism - 4th Edition: How White People Can Work for Racial Justice.* Gabriola Island: New Society Publishers, 2017.

Manning, Jennifer E. and Ida A. Brudnick. "Appendix. Total Number of Women Who Served in Each Congress." *Women in Congress - Statistics and Brief Overview, R43244 Version 30.* Washington DC: Congressional Research Service, December 4, 2020. p. 18. Accessed February 19, 2021. https://fas.org/sgp/crs/misc/R43244.pdf.

Murphy, Dan. "Ocasio-Cortez Not Proud of Westchester Roots." *Yonkers Times,* July 18, 2018. Accessed February 18, 2021. https://yonkerstimes.com/ocasio-cortez-not-proud-of-westchester-roots/.

Netroots Nation. "Speaker Profile Alexandria Ocasio-Cortez." Accessed February 18, 2021. https://www.netrootsnation.org/profile/alexandria-ocasio/.

Oxford University Press. s.v. "Microaggression." Accessed February 18, 2021. https://www.lexico.com/en/definition/microaggression.

Reitman, Eliza. "The Truth about Alexandria Ocasio-Cortez: The Inside Story of How, in Just One Year, Sandy the Bartender Became a Lawmaker Who Triggers Both Parties." *Insider (blog),* January 6, 2019. Accessed February 20, 2021. https://www.insider.com/alexandria-ocasio-cortez-biography-2019-1.

Ruiz, Michelle. "AOC's Next Four Years." *Vanity Fair,* October 28, 2020. Accessed April 5, 2021. https://www.vanityfair.com/news/2020/10/becoming-aoc-cover-story-2020.

Ruiz-Grossman, Sarah. "Alexandria Ocasio-Cortez Recounts Fear That She Was 'Going to Die' in Capitol Attack." *HuffPost* (blog), February 1, 2021. https://www.huffpost.com/entry/alexandria-ocasio-cortez-capitol-attack_n_601882e8c-5b6aa4bad36b2e4.

Steward, Andrew. "How Long Was Alexandria Ocasio-Cortez Planning Her Run for Public Office?" *Washington Babylon* (blog), August 28, 2018. Accessed February 20, 2021. https://washingtonbabylon.com/a-o-c-tweet-mccain/.

Weiss, Suzannah. "15 Microaggressions Women Face on a Daily Basis." *Bustle,* October 25, 2015. Accessed February 18. 2021. https://www.bustle.com/articles/119429-15-microaggressions-women-face-on-a-daily-basis-because-they-all-add-up-to-an-unequal.

Women Dignity Alliance. "Our Founder." About. Accessed February 16, 2021. https://www.womendignityalliance.com/our-founder.

Zhou, Li. "A Historic New Congress Will Be Sworn in Today." *Vox,* January 3, 2019. Accessed February 18, 2021. https://www.vox.com/2018/12/6/18119733/congress-diversity-women-election-good-news.

CHAPTER NINE

Abrams, Jasmine. "Blurring the Lines of Traditional Gender Roles: Beliefs of African American Women." (master's thesis, Virginia Commonwealth University, 2012). Accessed March 24, 2021. https://doi.org/10.25772/MEPQ-7539.

Behm, Don. "Pro Pot: Voters Support All Marijuana Advisory Referendums on Tuesday's Ballots." *Milwaukee Journal Sentinel,* updated on November 7, 2018. Accessed January 31, 2021. https://www.jsonline.com/story/news/politics/elections/2018/11/06/marijuana-legalization-milwaukee-county-voters-favor-ending-ban/1811494002/.

Bell, Ella L.J.E. and Stella M. Nkomo. *Our Separate Ways: Black and White Women and the Struggle for Professional Identity.* Brighton: Harvard Business Review Press, 2003.

Bernstein, Amy, Sarah Green Carmichael, and Nicole Torres. "Sisterhood Is Critical to Racial Justice." June 8, 2020. In *Women at Work.* Produced by Harvard Business Review. Podcast, MP3 audio, 1:05:10. https://hbr.org/podcast/2020/06/sisterhood-is-critical-to-racial-justice.

Bradt, Steve. "'One-Drop Rule' Persists." *Harvard Gazette,* December 6, 2010. Accessed March 24, 2021. https://news.harvard.edu/gazette/story/2010/12/one-drop-rule-persists/.

Brescoll, Victoria L. "Leading With Their Hearts? How Gender Stereotypes of Emotion Lead to Biased Evaluations of Female Leaders." *The Leadership Quarterly* Volume 27, Issue 3 (June 2016): 415-425. http://dx.doi.org/10.1016/j.leaqua.2016.02.005.

Center for Institutional Courage. "About Courage." Accessed March 25, 2021. https://www.institutionalcourage.org/about-us.

DiAngelo, Robin. *White Fragility: Why It's So Hard for White People to Talk About Racism.* Boston: Beacon Press, 2018.

Dill, Molly. "HaloVino to Introduce New Product." *BizTimes*, May 7, 2018. Accessed January 31, 2021. https://biztimes.com/halovino-to-introduce-new-product.

Glauber, Bill and Alison Durr. "Chris Larson, David Crowley Advance to April 7 Election in Milwaukee County Executive Race." *Milwaukee Journal Sentinal*, February 19, 2020. https://www.jsonline.com/story/news/politics/elections/2020/02/18/chris-larson-david-crowley-purnima-nath-theodore-lipscomb-sr/4790289002/.

Greater Milwaukee Foundation. "Home." Accessed January 31, 2021. https://www.greatermilwaukeefoundation.org/.

Halo Vino. "Home." Accessed January 31, 2021. https://halovino.com/.

Hurt, Jeanette. "Sommelier Develops Plastic Wine Glasses That Double as 'Good' Wine Glasses." *Forbes*, September 30, 2018. https://www.forbes.com/sites/jeanettehurt/2018/09/30/sommelier-develops-plastic-wine-glasses-that-double-as-good-wine-glasses/?sh=155ca9e315fe.

League of Women Voters of Wisconsin. "Women Who Inspire: Sharlen Moore." Member Spotlight. Accessed February 4, 2021. https://my.lwv.org/wisconsin/article/women-who-inspire-sharlen-moore.

Lumen Learning, s.v. "Social Institutions." Accessed March 29, 2021. https://courses.lumenlearning.com/wm-introductionto-sociology/chapter/reading-introduction-to-culture/.

MalamaDoe. "Book by Sheila Long." Accessed April 7, 2021. https://malamadoe.com/sheilalongauthor/.

Marley, Patrick. "Crisis at Lincoln Hills Juvenile Prison Years in Making." *Milwaukee Journal Sentinel,* December 17, 2016. Accessed February 5, 2021. https://www.jsonline.com/story/news/investigations/2016/12/17/crisis-lincoln-hills-juvenile-prison-years-making/95383518/.

Minority Rights. "Afro-Brazilians." Accessed March 24, 2021. https://minorityrights.org/minorities/afro-brazilians/.

Miyazaki Kevin J. and Mary Louise Schumacher. "Interview with Sharlen Moore." This is Milwaukee. Accessed April 10, 2021. https://www.thisismilwaukee.us/sharlenmoore.

Moore, Sharlen. "Lincoln Hills Closed. Now What's Needed?" *Urban Milwaukee,* August 28, 2018. Accessed February 5, 2021. https://urbanmilwaukee.com/2018/08/27/op-ed-after-lincoln-hills-closing-whats-needed/.

Negrón-Muntaner, Frances. "Are Brazilians Latinos? What Their Identity Struggle Tells Us about Race in America." *The Conversation,* December 20, 2016. Accessed March 24, 2021. https://theconversation.com/are-brazilians-latinos-what-their-identity-struggle-tells-us-about-race-in-america-64792.

On the Table. "Home." Accessed January 31, 2021. https://onthetablemke.org/.

Oxford University Press. s.v. "Culture." Accessed March 29, 2021. https://www.lexico.com/en/definition/culture.

Oxford University Press. s.v. "Miscegenation." Accessed March 24, 2021. https://www.lexico.com/en/definition/miscegenation.

Pew Research Center. "Chapter 3: The Multiracial Identity Gap." In *Multiracial in America: Proud, Diverse and Growing in Numbers,* edited by Kim Parker, Juliana Manasce Horowritz, Rich Morin, and Mark Hugo Lopez, 40-50. Washington, D.C.: 2015. https://www.pewresearch.org/social-trends/2015/06/11/multiracial-in-america/.

Pfeffer, Jeffrey. *Power Why People Some Have It and Others Don't.* New York City: Harper Business, 2010.

Urban Underground. "Impact." Join. Accessed January 31, 2021. https://www.urbanunderground.org/untitled-cc16.

WGTB. "Gov. Walker Calls for Closing of Lincoln Hills." *WGTD,* January 4, 2018. Accessed February 5, 2021. https://www.wgtd.org/news/gov-walker-calls-closing-lincoln-hills.

White, Laurel. "Walker Signs Law Closing Lincoln Hills Youth Prison." *Wisconsin Public Radio,* March 30, 2018. Accessed February 5, 2021. https://www.wpr.org/walker-signs-law-closing-lincoln-hills-youth-prison.

Wisconsin Foodie. "Home." Accessed January 31, 2021. https://www.wisconsinfoodie.com/.

YouthJusticeMKE. "Sharlen Celebrates Youth." October 23, 2018. Facebook video, 1:42. Accessed March 28, 2021. https://www.facebook.com/yjmke/posts/327684267814311.

CHAPTER TEN

Astia. "Home." Accessed January 30, 2021. https://www.astia.org/.

Ball, Molly. "How Nancy Pelosi Got to Congress." *Sabato's Crystall Ball UVA Center for Politics* (blog), May 8, 2020. Accessed January 30, 2021. https://centerforpolitics.org/crystalball/articles/how-nancy-pelosi-got-to-congress/.

Biographical Directory of the United States Congress. "Alesandro, Thomas, Jr." Biography. Accessed January 30, 2021. https://bioguide.congress.gov/search/bio/D000007.

Biographical Directory of the United States Congress. "Pelosi, Nancy." Biography. Accessed January 30, 2021. https://bioguide.congress.gov/search/bio/P000197.

Boudjadja, Meriem. Interview with author. August 21, 2020.

Center for American Women and Politics. "History of Women in the U.S. Congress." Rutgers Eagleton Institute of Politics. Accessed January 30, 2021. https://cawp.rutgers.edu/history-women-us-congress.

Chamorro-Premuzic, Tomás. "Why Do So Many Incompetent Men Become Leaders?" *Harvard Business Review*, August 22, 2013. Accessed March 20, 2021. https://hbr.org/2013/08/why-do-so-many-incompetent-men?.

Chang, Emily. *Brotopia: Breaking up the Boys' Club of Silicon Valley.* New York: Penguin Audio, 2018. Audible audio ed., 5 hr., 22 min.

Crewe, Lewis and Annie Wang. "Gender Inequalities in the City of London Advertising Industry." Abstract. *Environment and Planning A: Economy and Space 50,* no. 3 (May 2018). doi: 10.1177/0308518X17749731.

Equality Now (blog). "The United States Must Guarantee Equality on the Basis of Sex in the Constitution." July 2, 2020. Accessed on February 1, 2021. https://www.equalitynow.org/era_amicus_brief.

Feminist Majority. "Statement by Eleanor Smeal, President, Feminist Majority On the Equal Rights Amendment and the Violence Against Women Act." Feminist Majority press release, March 17, 2021. Feminist Majority Website. https://feministmajority.org/press/statement-by-eleanor-smeal-president-feminist-majority-on-the-equal-rights-amendment-and-the-violence-against-women-act/.

Finette, Jane. *Unlocked: How Empowered Women Empower Women.* Potomac: New Degree Press, 2021.

Grow, Jean M. and Tao Deng. "Time's Up/Advertising Meets *Red Books*: Hard Data and Women's Experiences Underscore the Pivotal Nature of 2018." *Journal of Current Issues & Research in Advertising.* (August 7, 2020): 5. https://doi.org/10.1080/10641734.2020.1753599.

Guillen, Laura. "Is the Confidence Gap between Men and Women a Myth?" *Harvard Business Review,* March 26, 2018. Accessed April 4, 2021. https://hbr.org/2018/03/is-the-confidence-gap-between-men-and-women-a-myth.

Harris, Russ and Steven Hayes. *The Confidence Gap: A Guide to Overcoming Fear and Self-Doubt*. Durban: Trumpeter: 2011.

Hart, Hanna. "The Confidence Gap Is A Myth, But A Double Standard Does Exist: How Women Can Navigate." *Forbes*, March 5, 2019. https://www.forbes.com/sites/hannahart/2019/03/05/the-confidence-gap-is-a-myth-but-a-double-standard-does-exist-how-women-can-navigate/.

Hickey, Walt and Mariana Alfaro, Grace Panetta, and Taylor Ardrey. "Nancy Pelosi Was Just Re-Elected as House Speaker — Here's How She Went from San Francisco Housewife to the Most Powerful Woman in Us Politics." *BusinessInsider.com*, January 3, 2021. Accessed January 30, 2021. https://www.businessinsider.com/nancy-pelosi-2013-3.

Ibarra, Herminia and Otilia Obodaru. "Women and the Vision Thing." *Harvard Business Review,* January 2009. Accessed March 20, 2021. https://hbr.org/2009/01/women-and-the-vision-thing.

Kay, Katty and Claire Shipman. *The Confidence Code: The Science and Art of Self-Assurance—What Women Should Know.* New York City: Harper Business, 2018.

Kay, Katty and Claire Shipman. "The Confidence Gap." *The Atlantic,* May 2014. Accessed April 4, 2021. https://www.theatlantic.com/magazine/archive/2014/05/the-confidence-gap/359815/.

Khanna, Pooja and Zachary Kimmel with Ravi Karkara. *Convention on the Elimination of All Forms of Discrimination Against Women (CEDAW) for Youth.* New York: *United Nations Entity for Gender Equality and the Empowerment of Women,* 2016. https://www.unwomen.org/-/media/headquarters/attach-ments/sections/library/publications/2016/cedaw-for-youth-brief.pdf?la=en&vs=1243.

Lindeman, Meghan I.H. and Amanda M. Durik, and Maura Dooley. "Women and Self-Promotion: A Test of Three Theories." *Psychological Reports* 122, no. 1 (February 2019): abstract, 219–30. https://doi.org/10.1177/0033294118755096.

MalamaDoe. "Book by Sheila Long." Accessed April 7, 2021. https://malamadoe.com/sheilalongauthor/.

McKinsey & Co. *Diversity Wins: How Inclusion Matters.* New York: McKinsey & Company, 2020. https://www.mckinsey.com/fea-tured-insights/diversity-and-inclusion/diversity-wins-how-in-clusion-matters.

Mozilla. "Mozilla Manifesto." About. Accessed April 4, 2021. https://www.mozilla.org/en-US/about/.

Nancy Pelosi Speaker of the House. "Pelosi Statement on 26th Anniversary of Violence Against Women Act." Nancy Pelosi Speaker of the House press release, September 13, 2020. Nancy Pelosi Speaker of the House website. https://www.speaker.gov/newsroom/91320.

TechTarget. "Firefox." Accessed April 6, 2021. https://whatis.techtarget.com/definition/Firefox.

The Coaching Fellowship. "About Us." Accessed January 30, 2021. https://www.tcfs.org/about/.

Times Up Now. "Our Work." Accessed January 30, 2021. https://timesupnow.org/work/.

UN Office of the High Commissioner for Human Rights (OHCHR). "20 years from the entry into force of the Optional Protocol to the Convention on the Elimination of All Forms of Discrimination against Women (OP-CEDAW): A universal instrument for upholding the rights of women and girls and for their effective access to justice." *United Nations Human Rights Council News*, December 10, 2020. Accessed April 11, 2021. https://www.ohchr.org/EN/HRBodies/HRC/Pages/NewsDetail.aspx?NewsID=26592&LangID=E.

Wray, Richard. "Ten Years after the Crash, the Dotcom Boom Can Finally Come of Age." *The Guardian*, March 23, 2010. https://www.theguardian.com/business/2010/mar/14/technology-dot-com-crash-2000.

CHAPTER ELEVEN

A Conscious Rethink (blog). "13 Signs You Have A Strong Personality That Might Scare Some People." Updated on August 22, 2019. Accessed March 17, 2021. https://www.aconsciousrethink.com/2925/13-signs-you-have-a-strong-personality-that-might-scare-some-people/.

American Express. The 2019 State of Women-Owned Business Report. New York: American Express, 2019. https://s1.q4cdn.com/692158879/files/doc_library/file/2019-state-of-women-owned-businesses-report.pdf.

Bartolomé, Fernando and Paul A. Lee Evans. "Why Must Success Cost So Much." *Harvard Business Review*, March 1980. https://hbr.org/1980/03/must-success-cost-so-much.

Cleise Brazilian Day Spa. "Welcome." Accessed February 21, 2021. https://cleisespa.com/.

Covey, Franklin. "Habit 1: Be Proactive." The 7 Habits of Highly Effective People. Accessed February 18, 2021. https://www.franklincovey.com/the-7-habits/habit-1/.

Covey, Steven R. *The 7 Habits of Highly Effective People: Powerful Lesson in Personal Change*. New York: Free Press, 2004.

Doyenne Group. "Our Mission." About Us. Accessed February 21, 2021. https://doyennegroup.org/about-us/mission.

Goldman Sachs. *Voice of Small Business in America: 2019 Insights Report*. New York: Goldman Sachs, 2019. https://www.goldmansachs.com/citizenship/10000-small-businesses/US/2019-insights-report/report.pdf.

Hispanic Chamber of Commerce of Wisconsin. "Home." Accessed March 17, 2021. https://hccw.org/.

Kiva. "Home." Accessed February 21, 2021. https://www.kiva.org/.

Kos, Blaze. "Healthy Relationships Are What Matters Most in Life." *Agile Lean Life* (blog). Accessed February 18, 2021. https://agileleanlife.com/healthy-relationships/.

Kos, Blaze. "Relationship Circles – the Most Important Diagram of Your Life." *AgileLeanLife* (blog). Accessed February 18, 2021. https://agileleanlife.com/relationship-circles/.

Milwaukee Area Technical College. "Home." Accessed February 21, 2021. https://www.matc.edu/.

Rowen, Dolores. *Veteran Women & Business: A Data Resource: Employing the U.S. Census Survey of Business Owners and Self-Employed Persons and the Annual Survey of Entrepreneurs to Develop a Profile of Veteran Women-Owned Firms.* Washington DC: National Women's Business Council, 2017. https://cdn.www.nwbc.gov/wp-content/uploads/2018/01/09084859/NWBC-Report_Veteran-Women-Business-A-Data-Resource.pdf.

Sherbinow, Michelle. Email message to author. February 22, 2021.

Small Business Administration. "Home." Accessed March 17, 2021. https://www.sba.gov/.

Spaulding Medical. "Home." Accessed February 21, 2021. https://spauldingmedical.com/.

Spaulding Medical. "Take ECGs In-Home." Accessed February 21, 2021. https://spauldingmedical.com/ecg-at-home-clinical-trials/.

United States Hispanic Chamber of Commerce. "Home." Accessed March 17, 2021. https://ushcc.com/.

WWBIC. "About WWBIC." Accessed February 21, 2021. https://www.wwbic.com/about-wwbic/.

WWBIC. "Home." Accessed February 21, 2021. https://www.wwbic.com/.

YWCA Southeast Wisconsin. "Home." Accessed February 21, 2021. https://www.ywcasew.org/about/mission-history/.

STORIES FROM WOMEN WHO INSPIRED ME

McNearney, Allison. "Watch Terrified Men Learn to Deal with Women in the Workforce During WWII." History Stories. Updated March 2, 2018. Accessed April 6, 2021. https://www.history.com/news/women-workforce-wwii-training-video-1940s.

Wallenfang, Maureen. "The Buzz: Fox River Mall turns 30." *The Post Crescent*, July 12, 2014. Accessed April 6, 2021. https://www.postcrescent.com/story/money/companies/buzz/2014/07/12/buzz-fox-river-mall/12534373/.

Made in the USA
Monee, IL
10 October 2021

79723191R00173